Berlin for Jews

Berlin for Jews

A Twenty-First-Century Companion

Leonard Barkan

The University of Chicago Press

Chicago and London

The University of Chicago Press, Chicago 60637
The University of Chicago Press, Ltd., London
© 2016 by The University of Chicago
All rights reserved. Published 2016.
Printed in the United States of America

25 24 23 22 21 20 19 18 17 16   1 2 3 4 5

ISBN-13: 978-0-226-01066-3 (cloth)
ISBN-13: 978-0-226-01083-0 (e-book)
DOI: 10.7208/chicago/9780226010830.001.0001

Library of Congress Cataloging-in-Publication Data
Names: Barkan, Leonard, author.
Title: Berlin for Jews : a twenty-first-century companion / Leonard Barkan.
Description: Chicago : The University of Chicago Press, 2016.
Identifiers: LCCN 2016005824 | ISBN 9780226010663 (cloth : alk. paper) | ISBN 9780226010830
   (e-book)
Subjects: LCSH: Jews, German–Germany–Berlin–History. | Jews, German–Germany–Berlin–
   Biography. | Varnhagen, Rahel, 1771–1833. | Benjamin, Walter, 1892–1940. | Simon, James,
   1851–1932. | Berlin (Germany) –Description and travel.
Classification: LCC DS134.3 .B37 2016 | DDC 943/.155004924–dc23 LC record available at http://
   lccn.loc.gov/2016005824

⊖ This paper meets the requirements of
ANSI/NISO Z39.48-1992 (Permanence of Paper).

In grateful recognition of a whole generation of exiles who were my teachers, whether in person or by example. I think especially of three remarkable individuals who taught me German: at Horace Mann, Arthur F. Walber from Bottrop (1897–1991); at Swarthmore, Hilde Cohn from Görlitz (1909–2001) and Franz Mautner from Vienna (1902–1995).

What a glorious slap in the face of evil that all three lived to such a grand age in their adopted homeland!

Contents

Prologue: **Me and Berlin**

The first time I entered into psychotherapy, traumatized by a love affair that didn't happen and by separation anxiety when I was forced to leave the East Coast for Southern California, I was determined to be a good patient and tell the truth. So at the very start, I announced that there were three secrets so terrible and private that I had to get them off my chest immediately, lest I never arrive at real honesty with the doctor. I polished off homosexuality and masturbation lickety-split. But when I came to the third secret, despite all my lofty determination, I was struck dumb, and I spent the rest of the session—and several more sessions—beating around this particular burning bush. The secret was that I had often pretended I wasn't a Jew.

Let me take that apart. First of all, I *am* a Jew, 100% Ashkenazi (actually, 93% by official DNA count, thanks to Ancestry.com) in the most standard manner imaginable: Litvak, Ellis Island, Lower East Side, enthusiastic consumer of gefilte fish and pastrami, knishes and belly lox, not necessarily at the same time. My largest claim to distinction within this vast archetype, I suppose, is that my family was passionately antireligious. The only Jewish ritual in which I ever took part happened to me at the age of eight days (they were resentfully placating some grandparent or other), and I'm glad to say I have no recollection of it. But my family's militant secularism is its own kind of stereotype—not the last time we'll hear about that phenomenon in these pages—and so it hardly frees me from the Jewish mainstream.

Now about that pretending. Why did I do it? There were, as they say in the social sciences, push factors and pull factors. The pull factors are easy: J. S. Bach, John Milton, Piero della Francesca. The truth is, I have never quite learned how to love great art without believing what it says. The push factors are a far more delicate subject. I suppose that, like children everywhere,

I was becoming a mutant version of my parents. Having made the great leap from shtetl poverty to the Manhattan middle class, from Eastern European polyglot to elocution-teacher English, from rabbinical orthodoxy to left-wing secularism, they didn't look back. Or rather, they looked back often, but with disapproval, with self-congratulatory relief, and (especially) with mockery. That was their gig; as for me, faced with all that disagreeable baggage, I simply checked it and threw away the key.

My double life—and that's what it was, since I could hardly mix my WASP personality transplant with a home life full of latkes, sarcasm, and jokes about Tish Ba'av—might be said to have climaxed, and eventually dissolved, in my attendance at a High Anglican church in New Haven that outdid all others in a race to imitate the rituals of something like twelfth-century Catholicism: holy water, stations of the cross, miasmas of incense, and a stray nun, left over perhaps from some monastic foundation that didn't get the memo when Henry VIII shut them down. The vibrantly berobed figure who presided over this medieval spectacle was one Father Kibitz, a converted Jew. (That's his real name. I couldn't invent a better one, so, *alav ha shalom*, he must be identified here.) I'm not sure I ever exchanged a word with him, but I spent numerous Sunday mornings in the thrall of his sacred spectacle.

I should say, to Father Kibitz's credit, that unlike me he concealed nothing about his origins. (He couldn't have: his nose and his Bronx accent would have made it impossible. But perhaps I was just as transparent.) It must have been some combination of seeing him and seeing myself, along with the more pedestrian fact that I was about to begin a new life three thousand miles away, and therefore free to dis-reinvent myself, that caused my whole impersonation simply to evaporate.

Once the air cleared, I began to realize just what kind of Jew I was. I had grown up in New York, I had a considerable vocabulary of Yiddish, I loved poems and paintings and symphonies, but saw no contradiction in loving the Marx Brothers just as much, I devoured starchy comfort food and spicy irony with equal enthusiasm. There were just two things that I didn't do. I couldn't see myself graduating from the theater of Father Kibitz to that of ten years ago, fallen in love-at-first-sight with Berlin. Mind you, I wasn't one of those Jews who refused to go to Germany: over the years I had visited Goethe's house in Frankfurt, sung "Die Lorelei" *auf Deutsch* while passing her legendary rock during my personal Siegfried Idyll of a Rhine journey, gazed at ancient sculpture in Munich's Glyptothek, and tasted Riesling on the banks of the Mosel. In fact, courtesy of all those A pluses in German class, I was selected as an exchange student from my high school to the Schadowschule in West Berlin, except that the year was 1961, the Soviets had started to build The Wall, and no little boys from New York were going to be shipped off to that particular theater of the Cold War. Germany itself was no problem—if it is a problem for you, dear reader, I've written this book with precisely you in mind—I just hadn't ventured as far east as the Capital City.

When I did venture there, along with my spouse, it was in the midst of a year's residence in Italy, a circumstance almost fictional in its appropriateness, since Rome had through several decades of my adult life been the official adopted home, fostering a sense of my origins in the manner named by Freud as "the family romance"—children's practice of inventing alternative parents, generally of higher social standing, from whom they have been abducted by the pair of ordinary schmoes who tuck them into bed at night. Rome wasn't exactly my fantasy parent, and I never pretended to be an Italian, though I was occasionally mistaken for one. But when I took that momentous flight from Fiumicino to Schoenefeld, it turned out I was finding a second second home.

Mind you, if I am sending you on this quest for Berlin, it's not just about the Jewish thing. Of course you know that Berlin is fascinating. I don't need to tell you about visiting Museum Island and the Brandenburg Gate, about the ever-expanding arts scene in Mitte, Neukölln, Friedrichshain, and further gentrifying points east, not to mention the twee scene in Prenzlauer Berg (fight your way through the baby carriages to a sublime selection of cafés, galleries, and quaint street scenes). You may also be eager to do the Cold War tour—Checkpoint Charlie, the Stasi Museum, the Gedenkstätte der Berliner Mauer, etc., even if it leaves me a little, well, cold, since I'm always wondering, if they were so hungry for freedom as to risk their lives by evading The Wall in 1965, where was that hunger for freedom thirty years earlier? But let's not go there, *yet*.

Here's where you *should* go, to begin with. Go buy a transit pass for whatever unit of time you'll be in Berlin; the AB sectors should be sufficient. They are extremely good value, since they allow you unlimited access to one of the world's greatest transportation systems: swift, efficient, and, most important of all, beautifully integrated, so that you have a kind of seamless access across trains, buses, trams, and—yes!—even ferries (remember, Berlin is surrounded by lakes). Every stop of every conveyance lets you know what other conveyances are nearby and often tells you how long you'll wait until the next one appears, predictions that (with certain memorable exceptions) tend to be precise to the minute. I don't know any other city—certainly not my beloved hometown—where public transportation gives you such a complete sense that the urban world belongs to you.

And here, by way of a beginning, is what you should do with all this freedom. Ride the bus. There are well-known routes—100 and 200—made for tourism and focusing on locations like Unter den Linden, Potsdamer Platz, and the Victory Column. Well and good, but I'll be directing you, transit pass in hand, elsewhere.

Take the U-Bahn to Hermannplatz, which is the end (or, in your case, the beginning) of the M29 bus line. You'll begin in a Kreuzberg neighborhood that is raffish, even louche, but bustling with multicultural enterprise (Figure 0. 1), and, later, when you step off the bus, you'll almost feel you're in the country (Figure 0. 2). In between you'll pass bucolic waterways lined with grand (sometimes, *once* grand) residences, you'll stake out the Jewish Museum and the Berlinische Galerie, as well as two of the world's great cultural institutions: the Gemäldegalerie and the Philharmonie (for my money, the perfect concert hall). Traversing the newspaper district, you'll pass the mooring point of *Die Welt's* hot air balloon and the decapitated-looking sculpted heads of Helmut Kohl, Mikhail Gorbachev, and George H. W. Bush that adorn the headquarters of Axel Springer's journalistic empire. You'll see Checkpoint Charlie and a bit of The Wall. As an antidote to all that DDR-ish East, you'll travel quite a few

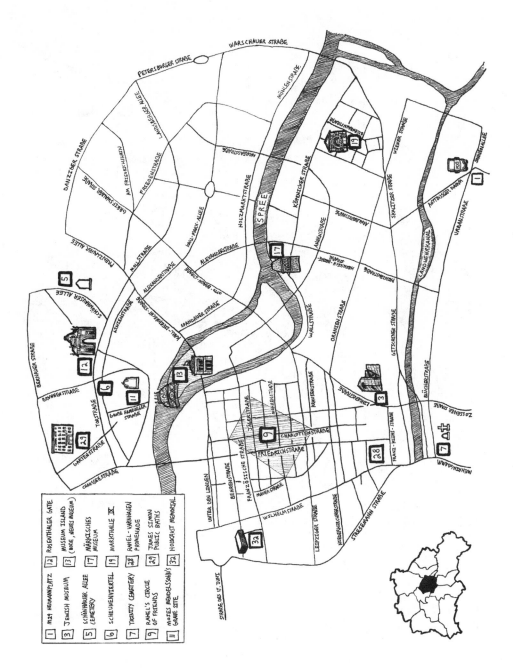

Berlin East and Center

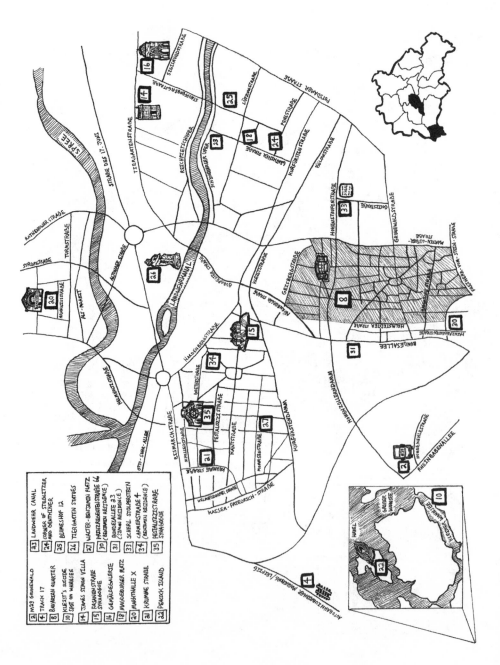

Berlin West

blocks of Kurfürstendamm, mecca of international shopping. You'll see the carefully preserved ruins of the Anhalter Bahnhof and the Gedächtniskirche. And just opposite that majestic pile, you'll be able to take note, for subsequent mealtime enjoyment, of KaDeWe (Kaufhaus des Westens), with its wonderfully named *Feinschmecker* Floor (see? You already know some German), a labyrinth of deliciousness for the gourmet. At the end, you'll find yourself among the spectacularly grand early twentieth-century residences of Grunewald, which seem to have escaped catastrophe, or to have risen intact from it.

It's only been an hour, so you'll have plenty of time to dig deeper into the city. You'll have some agonizing choices, to be sure. Three full-time opera companies vs. enough alternative entertainment to cripple a hipster. The weeping willow–banked canals in Kreuzberg vs. the lake at Alt-Tegel, which is five minutes' walk from what remains of a nineteenth-century market hall filled with the very best twenty-first-century foodstuffs. Dancing to the music supplied by an ever-inventive DJ (Wednesday is tango night!) on the banks of the Spree with the backdrop of the beautiful Bode Museum as warm weather entertainment (Figure 0. 3), or, in cold weather, visiting one of the Christmas markets where edibles, drinkables, and trinkets will make it forever clear to you why *kitsch* is a German word.

Admiring blocks and blocks of beautiful nineteenth-century domestic architecture—can that structure have survived 1945? or did they really go to the trouble of reassembling every one of those sixteen belle epoque tchotchkes on a structure that functions as nothing grander than a standard issue six-flat? (Figure 0. 4)—will have to leave you some time to be fascinated by an assemblage of modern apartment blocks, on a design plan somewhere between Gaudi and Peter Rabbit, courtesy of the Baller family of architects, and sprinkled throughout the city. Enjoying Kürbisfest (thirty different shapes and flavors of squash) in the fall and Spargelfest (white asparagus, after one taste of which you will never buy that product again outside of Germany) in the spring, not to mention the brightly colored strawberry-shaped tin huts (Figure 0.5) that sprout up, also seasonally, in all the major U-Bahn and S-Bahn stations offering not only baskets of strawberries but also an aroma of spring permeating the whole transit system.

You'll have to decide in what order to track down the secret parks: we followed a path between perfectly ordinary apartment houses in an especially nondescript corner of the crowded Tiergarten neighborhood only to find ourselves at a little hidden lake whose sole inhabitant was a heron flexing its massive wingspan. Or to explore the hidden courtyards (try Kreuzberg in particular), where you can penetrate ever deeper into sanctums of architecture in a half dozen different styles, often within the same structure.

No, you don't have to be Jewish to love Berlin.

On the other hand, I *am* Jewish. And I can't send you on this Berlin journey without acknowledging the perils. I'm not talking about personal safety, or threats to your budget, or boredom: Berlin is, in fact, safe, economical, and fun for all ages. Permit me, however, to quote from my journal, as my spouse and I spent the summer of 2011 in the city we had already come to love:

> A walkthrough of the German Historical Museum has nearly aborted the project of writing the book. A friend of mine, herself a lover of Berlin and a Jew like me but with an impeccable genealogy going back to high bourgeois Weimar Republic intelligentsia *unlike* me, once issued a stern warning about our shared enthusiasm. A friend of hers, it seems, would insist every time she reached a certain peak of encomia in regard to the city that she take a trip to Track 17 at the Grunewald S-Bahn station [we'll hear more about this in the epilogue to this book] and walk along those dismal milestones detailing the number of Jews shipped off, day by day, to the extermination camps. "Remember," he would say to her, "that's where it all ended." I had, in fact, walked that walk on several occasions; and I certainly got the message, but, perhaps because of the simplicity and beauty of the medium in which the message is delivered at Track 17, I was always able to integrate it into my own warm and fuzzy complex of sentiments about the city.
>
> The materials on view at the German Historical Museum [a show about the Berlin police during the Nazi period] can't really

claim simplicity or beauty. They are brutal and unsparing: interviews with victims of torture; sequences of terrible punishments meted out to Jews, Roma people, Homosexuals, and resisters of the regime; a giant replica of Auschwitz [this last bit of the exhibition I turned my back on]. Staggering through all this, Nick says to me, "Germany is in A.A. To get sober, it has to tell the story of its crimes over and over again." The quip is delightful and disturbing, in familiar proportions. But I have no quips about what I have seen during these ninety minutes. It certainly isn't the first time my nose has been rubbed in Nazi atrocity. I grew up, after all, in a heavily Jewish milieu living out the immediate postwar years; and, though I cannot and will not claim personal ties to the millions of victims, the reminders of what we had been fighting for, the photographs of the dead, the nightmare narratives, whether real or cinematic, were fundamental cultural property to anyone like me born in 1944. If all that didn't stop me from learning German, from taking many wine tasting trips to the Mosel, and, above all, from my now passionate engagement with the Nazi capital city, why should ninety minutes in the German Historical Museum stop me in my tracks? The answer is a simple one: only now was I seriously thinking about writing this book, about taking my Berlin love affair public. . . .

Love affair is another figure of speech, like Germany in A.A., and Nick is once again quick with the metaphoric possibilities: "Is it a sentimental love affair? An unrequited love affair? An abusive love affair?"

Now, I guess, I would choose the term *tragic*. I have spent much of my professional life, as a literary scholar, thinking about Shakespearean tragedy. The heroes of those dramas are sometimes fundamentally good people (Hamlet), sometimes a mixture of good and bad (Othello, Lear), and sometimes pretty thoroughly bad (Macbeth). And yet we are gripped by all their fates, and, to one extent or another, we mourn them all. Berlin is just such a tragic hero: I am gripped by the city, and I mourn all the destructions, whether of persons, places, or cultures—those inflicted *by* Berlin and those inflicted *on* Berlin (which were, come to think of it, *also* inflicted *by* Berlin). On the other hand, Shakespeare's tragedies nearly always end with some glimmer of future hope. This book aspires to be a tentative in that direction.

What follows, then, is neither a complete history nor a complete itinerary—there are many fine volumes with those ambitions—but rather a set of portraits. Two places and three persons cannot cover the full space and time of that fascinating overlap between the circle of Berlin and the circle of Jews. But with its chapters on two locations, contrasting in geography, temporality, and purpose, followed by chapters on three remarkable individuals, born in the eighteenth, the mid-nineteenth, and the late nineteenth centuries, I hope that this volume can say something to the twenty-first century. For the travel-minded, the "Places" chapters will look more like itineraries and the "People" chapters more like histories. In fact, the book hopes to offer a convergence. If it coaxes a few persons into a willingness to visit, or if, when placed in the hands of the actual, the prospective, or the virtual voyager, it provides some informative companionship, it will have pleased me to make my Berlin love affair public.

I

Places: **Schönhauser Allee**

For those who seek the body and soul of Jewish Berlin, whether on foot or in guidebooks, ground zero tends to be pinpointed in the Scheunenviertel, or "Barn Quarter," named for a proliferation of structures that once kept highly flammable hay, as well as some less than desirable inhabitants, away from center city. It's a neighborhood within the larger outlines of Mitte that stretches from Rosa-Luxemburg-Platz westward, and it certainly qualifies for such a community-defining status. Within this square mile we find some of the earliest authorized settlements of Jews in the metropolis; and, not far into this period of history, we can locate the entrance point into Berlin of the fourteen-year-old beggar-student Moses Mendelssohn. Through the nineteenth century, it was the immigrant zone par excellence for the Ostjuden, immigrants from the East, after Berlin's middle- and upper-class Jews had succeeded in leaving such oriental traces behind them. And—presumably uniting the opposite ends of the social spectrum—it became the site for the Neue Sinagoge when that grandiose building was constructed on Oranienburger Straße in the 1860s.

The visitor of today, to be sure, won't want to miss this densely packed urban fabric of reclaimed Jewishness: not only the Synagogue (nowadays, only incidentally a synagogue, and principally a museum), but also the remains of Jewish schools and hospitals, and an early extant, or barely extant, graveyard, which includes an approximation of Moses Mendelssohn's resting place. How pleasant as well that the same neighborhood is ablaze with contemporary art galleries, intriguingly alternative eateries, and chic clothing boutiques. Indeed, one can visit the beautiful 1920s building in the "New Objectivity" style that once housed the Jewish Girls' School, and find it now transformed into several floors of art installations cohabiting with a fashion forward contemporary restaurant and an ersatz New York deli serving gray replicas of matzo balls.

Not that any of these twenty-first-century ironies, or *Der Spiegel's* droll announcement of the building's inauguration— "Warhol und Pastrami *to go*"—should be allowed to detract from the historical primacy of the Scheunenviertel. Be that as it may, my travelogue does not begin there, seeking instead some corners of the city where the heritage feels a little less commodified and a little more alive.

Okay, so "alive" is going to turn a little ironic when I reveal that one of my candidates for Jewish ground zero is, in fact, a cemetery. We'll return to those paradoxes anon; for the moment, though, let it be said that there are two epicenters in my own Jewish Berlin: one is in the East, the other in the West, one reflects Berlin in the nineteenth century, the other in the twentieth; one is a place where people lived, the other where they were laid to rest.

If I choose death before life, it is for the simple reason that the idea of writing this book came to me—not exactly full-blown, but with stunningly focused effect—at the moment when I first entered the Schönhauser Allee Jewish burial ground. What I was expecting, as I passed through the little iron gate of the cemetery and donned the obligatory loaner yarmulke, was nothing very uplifting: here, after all, was a graveyard that had witnessed a century or so of history before 1933, then the unspeakable annihilations sponsored by Nazi terror, then the decimations of total war that reduced the city to rubble, then forty or so years of stewardship under the DDR, presumably no special protector of imperial history or religious observance. What I saw, however, was a landscape of serene elegiac beauty. There were, to be sure, a goodly number of tumbled and even crumbled gravestones, though whether it was owing to the Holocaust or bombing raids or simply the ravages of time I couldn't tell. But I also felt that I had entered upon the gracious memorial garden of a particular past in which proud, well-to-do, and accomplished Jews had staked their claim on the civilization of a great city (Figure 1.1).

Why, precisely, was I so struck? My Manhattan upbringing,

to begin with, did not prepare me for the notion of a center-city graveyard. Granted, there are a few historic burial grounds with ancient, barely legible markers wedged in among the brownstones of Greenwich Village or the high-rises of the Financial District. But where I grew up it is unimaginable to find the kind of commemorative space where generations of the local citizenry have been interred and where a visitor of today can swiftly exit from the density of the urban landscape and take a bucolic stroll down this sort of memory lane. That would require, by my count, 29 stops on the Lexington Avenue IRT, for Woodlawn, and God only knows how long a ride into the terra incognita of Queens, for the many such sites located in that spacious borough. A fact brought home to me many years ago when the limo returning us in blistering heat from my father's interment broke down on the L.I.E. very far from any alternative transportation; I'm happy to report that when the hired rabbi, unknown to any of us before that moment since we were a decidedly rabbi-less family, lost all semblance of his unctuous clerical dignity and turned nasty in the face of this inconvenience to his pastoral schedule, my mother and I both got the giggles. Nor is this set of geographical arrangements merely a new world phenomenon: famous European cemeteries like Highgate and Père Lachaise are also tucked rather far from town centers.

Less so Berlin. There are, of course, important burial grounds at remote corners of the map, including the monumental successor to Schönhauser Allee, Friedhof Weissensee, said to be the largest Jewish resting place in Europe. (Like the Scheunenviertel, it has interested other chroniclers of Jewish Berlin more than it has interested me, though if you have three or four days to spare you can attempt to walk its perimeter.) But it is also possible to come across a considerable number of cemeteries, of all faiths, by taking the briefest of detours off the urban grid. I commend the St. Matthäus Kirchhof, scarcely five minutes' walk from the gritty Yorckstraße S-Bahn station, where you can see the identical tombstones of the Grimm Brothers lined up in a row; whether this regimented formation appears ominous or comical may depend on one's mood. Or, if you can tear yourself away from the hectic café life of Bergmannstraße, it takes only moments to enter a complex of Kreuzberg Protestant burial grounds and do as I did, which was to place memorial pebbles on the graves of Felix and Fanny Mendelssohn—a microscopic act of protest against their family conversion. (I was disappointed at not being the first to commit this little sacrilege: my contribution joined a sizeable pile of previous such ritual interventions.)

So, if we are to understand the stunning effect of entering Schönhauser Allee, it's best to begin with the experience of radical contrast. You are likely to approach the place having ridden the U-Bahn two stops beyond Alexanderplatz, than which nothing could be more urban in (literally) the most concrete sense. At the beginning of the short walk from the underground, you'll find a little triangle of pathetic greenery amusing only because the statue of Alois Senefelder, to whom the space is dedicated, records his name in mirror-writing, thus honoring his status as the inventor of lithography. At the end of the walk, quite obscuring the destination itself, there was for years a supremely ugly construction site, which only very recently has given way to some luxury condos wedged up against the hallowed space itself. In the middle, you'll be passing the rarest, though not the sweetest, of Berlin monuments: a cute little octagonal nineteenth-century pissoir, in burnished green metal and, I'm grateful to report from frequent experience, in perfect working order.

You may be ready, in other words, for something a little more uplifting. The pay-off, I'm afraid, is not instantaneous, as you proceed past the yarmulke dispensary and the admonitory welcoming inscription ("Here you keep silent, but when you leave, keep silent no more!"), and make your way through a tangle of garden tools and Dumpsters that often block one's first view of the gravesites themselves. Soon, though, this is all behind you, and all I can say is that at that point, on my first visit and ever after, I felt as though I had traveled to another climate. The Schönhauser Allee cemetery has, I discovered over many visits, two seasons. Either there are hints of brilliant sun dappled into radical oppositions of light and shade by the density of forestation, or else there is a uniform ashen hue of steel, rendering sky and boughs completely indistinct as the winds send the tree trunks into harmonic motion. I'm not talking about summer and winter here: in fact, the density of nature that confronts the visitor immediately upon entering its pathways is so overwhelming that it matters rather little whether the canopy of leaves is verdant, or golden, or fallen in amber hues to the ground, or wasted into a snow-covered powder. Indeed, I frequently encountered the two seasons within a quarter of an hour.

One reason for this seeming defiance of the round of the year, and for the impression that one has entered primordial nature, is that the whole space is governed by ivy (Figure 1.2). Swaths of erstwhile pathways are now packed in vine—not just a layer of tendrils but a veritable memory foam of creepers. Where ivy is choked out of groundspace, it climbs tree trunks. And since the trees are too tall for the vines to conquer, they have sought altitude, whether in the grandest or the humblest corners of the cemetery, by mounting the graves themselves. The result offers a surprising variety of decorative shapes: truncated stones that barely manage to raise their heads above the choking ground cover, others proudly erect but their contours and inscriptions completely obscured by a perfectly form-fitting coat of greenery, making them seem like lapidary forest people, still others fully visible and readable but decorated by a strand or two of vine, often on a rakish diagonal, as though smartly decked out for some woodland senior prom. Where the ivy stops, the moss begins. It, too, covers pathways and stones; it, too, ranges from complete wraparound enclosure of the memorials to elegant grace notes of decor.

I'm sure I was struck that first time—I'm not a late twentieth-century trained literature professor for nothing—by the fact that there is something almost embarrassingly, overdeterminedly metaphorical about the visual ensemble. Many of the stones feature actual sculpted ivy garlands—some now barely visible among the *real* garlands—as part of their aesthetic, while others are designedly rusticated, conceived in craggy boulder shapes that have been artfully mutilated by representations of creeping nature, and still others incorporate tiny marble-enclosed garden plots, summoning live greenery into the display itself, an invitation to which the decades have responded enthusiastically. Not to mention that one of these enshrines a family (a quite important family, as it happens) with the name MOSSE. God's pun on death.

So, with all this quietude and a color spectrum as intense as it is narrow—evergreen and ever-gray, sometimes sequentially, sometimes simultaneously—the space of Schönhauser Allee slaps you in the face with time-honored reflections under such rubrics as "memento mori" or "sic transit gloria mundi." Not to mention the nearly infinite number of set-ups for possible touristical snapshots, where crumbling sandstone morphs seamlessly into dead tree trunks or where marble shards are composed such that one can piece out fragments of the German for "deeply beloved Grandfather."

But right from that first visit this particular line of graveyard profundities gained no hold over my imagination. The whole Gray's "Elegy" thing, in fact, went out the window. That poetic masterpiece, to which Hardy owes "far from the madding crowd" and Kubrick "paths of glory," nailed down for centuries what it meant to muse on the long buried dead while gazing at their tombstones. But this book of mine would never have been born in a country churchyard. Gray's dead people were humble and nameless, "mute inglorious Miltons," flowers "born to blush unseen" with "homely joys and destiny obscure." The poet saunters among them, taking for granted that he can't know their names or their lives; and I'm not sure he cares.

I had, and have, other plans. Somehow, and double quick, I got past all those living metaphors of moss and ivy and the crumbled past, of *dust thou art, unto dust thou shalt return*. As I began to study the monuments, moving through this broad triangular space comprising something like five city blocks, broken by pathways into rectangles, sometimes trapezoids, of varying size, the whole ensemble created in the 1820s and in regular use until the early twentieth century, I swerved from elegy to archaeology. I began to ask—with, at first, no more erudition than my own eyes and my own imagination—what I might learn about this lost tribe from reading the gravestones, if I imagined them as the half-buried remnants of an unknown city. Which is exactly what they are.

There's plenty for an assiduous reader to absorb. The eyes of *this* assiduous reader, for example, given that he was well into his seventh decade, were drawn magnetically to the years of birth and death. A notably long-lived tribe, it seems. "Frau Emilie Hüterbock . . . Born 18 June 1811, died 19 March 1899": that math was particularly easy. "Amalie Cohen, née Engel, 9 April 1843–23 September 1929"; that's good: Engel was my grandmother's maiden name. "Sara Katz 16 September 1829–2 March 1898": my mother was a Katz, but this lifespan narrows in a little too closely on my own. And the winner:

> HIER RUHT
>
> NEBEN SEINER TREUEN FRAU
>
> DER FRÜHERE GÜRTLERMSTR
>
> M. FÜRSTENHEIM
>
> GEB. D. 5ten JANUAR 1818
>
> GEST. D. 7ten JANUAR 1917

Dazzled by longevity, I didn't pause to ask why no first name or what a former *Gürtlermeister* might be. On the other hand, my eye soon lit upon "Berline Schneider, 10 March 1851–3 February 1852."

But letters may prove more articulate than numbers. Names, to begin with. Schönhauser Allee is like a thesaurus of Jewish family names, a potential secret weapon in the lifelong quest to know who is Jewish, who isn't, and who's in hiding. Not that these tombstones nail the matter shut. There are, of course, *Cohen*s and *Levy*s and *Solomon*s. And you could probably call half the roll of my third grade class by just reading off some of these markers: *Jacobi, Blumenthal, Jacobson, Horwitz*. That class was taught by a Miss *Gans*, a name also represented here. (She claimed to be Scandinavian, but my mother had suspicions.) But what to do with *Fabian* or *Paradies*, and what about *Werther*, redolent of Goethe, or *Burg*, which puts me in mind of Luther's "Ein' feste Burg . . . ," or *Hagen*, right out of Wagner's *Ring*? Or echoes of other great, indisputably non-Semitic German writers, like *Leibnitz* and *Lessing*? The truth is that we identify Jews by their surnames, but we have to learn that they are, as the postmoderns say, *constructed*. Literally so; after all, some of this cemetery's in-habitants lived only a couple of generations past the time when Jews had the privilege—or was it compulsion?—of assuming sur-names, which had to be fabricated for the occasion.

The information on the stones yields other, perhaps more substantial, clues. I began to notice some stray indicators of where these people came from and where they were going. Quite a few graves tell us the deceased's birthplace, and, though many of those cite Berlin, a larger number make reference to quite dif-ferent origins. They are designated in German, but nowadays we know these places under names that are (at least for me) much more difficult to pronounce: Pyrzce; Mirosławiec; Zduny; Chojna; Szczecin. It all happened in the lifespan of one individ-ual; they were born Polish Jews, they died Berliners. And just what kind of Berliners they were—both the eastern immigrants and those whose families had made that trek earlier—we can also read on their tombstones, where a riot of majestic titles gets enumerated: *Justizrat, Professor an der Universität, Königlicher Com-merzenrath, Überregierungsrat, Amtgerichtsrat Professor*. The very fact that I have no idea what some of these grandiose and for-gotten tokens of honor signify only makes them, and their pos-sessors, the more lordly.

Of course, from the shtetl to the *Amtgerichtsrat* is an old story, but you don't have to look very far, in Schönhauser Allee or else-where, to notice the undertow in this surge. Just when you are about to marvel at (or, if you have tastes different from mine, bewail) the vast project of assimilation represented by these stately monuments, you are struck by the fact that a certain no-table proportion of the writing is in Hebrew. Which makes me an unreliable narrator. The not very rebellious child of anticlerical parents who would sooner have noshed on a raw pork knuckle than ship me off to bar mitzvah school, I seem to have cultivated four or five foreign tongues, ancient and modern, in the course of my life without the language of the Bible even making it onto the waiting list.

For me, then, the Hebrew isn't exactly language at all, some-thing more like hieroglyphic symbolism. Granted, some of it exists in a kind of interlinear with comprehensible text: *blah blah*

blah blah (or should I say *halb halb halb halb*?) SARA DOBRINER
NÉE BERNDT BORN MÄRK-FRIEDLAND . . . , which has the Rosetta
Stone potential of teaching me to translate if only I had any inclination that way. And, illiterate that I am, I do begin to notice
an expression almost universally incised amidst the Hebrew:
תנצבה ("May his or her soul be bound up in the bonds of eternal
life"). But there is something far more arresting than the semi-
otically ordinary business of one language yielding another.
From several vantage points in Schönhauser Allee, your gaze
falls upon a field of graves, all of grey sandstone, whose characters are largely effaced by the elements, except that you can
make out the remnants of line after line of Hebrew inscription
(Figures 1.3, 1.4). With this constricted focus, it's as though the
Roman alphabet hasn't been invented yet. In truth, my impression isn't alphabetic at all. Owing to a couple centuries of what
must be repeated meteorologic conditions, this helter-skelter
subset of ancient burial markers bears an imprint of what looks
like an ashen whirlwind, almost, but not quite, engulfing the
inscriptions.

So much for what the Hebrew means, or doesn't mean, to *me*.
Imagining what it meant to *them* requires a broader lens. To begin
with, the effect on that little sector of stones emblazoned (in my
imagination) with the whirlwind is more than an accident: these
graves mark some of the cemetery's earliest interments, and they
were made of notably unstable matter, whether because of poverty or because of an orthodox tradition that urges simplicity
and uniformity in the markers of the dead—a tradition extravagantly flaunted elsewhere in the cemetery. So, no surprise that
Hebrew goes with ancient, poor, and pious.

But not necessarily, it turns out. Among many of the grander
monuments, more recent and constructed out of ostentatiously
enduring substances, Hebrew stakes its own energetic claim,
generally given lead billing, providing (I can only assume) all
the necessary mortuary information at the head of the stone,
followed by the same in German. Far more often, though, the
scheme is German on one side of the stone, Hebrew on the other,
like some sort of dual language book that you can open either
from the back or the front. Is there a pattern to this double-faced

inscription? Does the Hebrew side face Jerusalem? Are they hoping that God reads from the back of the book? What it says to me is that this grand Berliner bourgeoisie wishes, when it contemplates life *sub specie aeternitatis*, to hedge its bets, to leave no stone unturned.

As witness a particularly amphibious inscription:

> LUDWIG BEER
> GEBOREN ZU BERLIN
> DEN 10 MAERZ 5581
> GESTORBEN ZU TEPLITZ
> DEN 20 SEPTEMBER 5591

The family of this poor deceased ten-year-old was clearly on the fence, and so created a little ecumenical hybrid, in effect, a monster. The Hebrew calendar, lunar rather than solar, has its own months and its own new year. 5581 had no March, only an *Adar* (actually, two *Adars*, an anomaly from following the moon rather than the sun—but let that pass). "10 March 5581" doesn't really mean anything, except as part of an energetic campaign to belong in two worlds at once.

But reading the stones, one has no doubt that these individuals, whatever ancient rituals they chose to summon up in the presence of death, felt at home in this land and in this language. I peruse these writings with the eye of an experienced close reader. I notice the tendency of the very short-lived to be memorialized in very long poems; I notice the man who died at age 78 and who gets praised for having worked hard in grade school. I especially take note of a quite original production: rhyming verses celebrating one decedent's Strength of Will (it's irresistible to replicate those German capital letters) and his Gentleness, his relief that he need no longer weep over his dead wife, since he is now as dead as she is, and his confidence that his son and apprentices will carry on his business. The whole thing, you notice on second glance, is composed such that the left-hand margin is an acrostic for his name. Except that the name is fifteen letters long, and poetic inspiration seems to have failed at line twelve, so the acrostic gets written out as follows:

G

E

R

S

O

N

B

E

R

N

ST

EIN

I pause longer, though, at a different textual ensemble. It's one of the simplest of the graves, one of the most recent, and to understand why it carries such an effect you have to do a little outside reading as well.

PROF. DR.

HEINRICH SILBERGLEIT

GEB. 2. 7. 1858 IN GLEIWITZ

GEST. 15. 3. 1939 IN BERLIN

EDEL SEI DER MENSCH,

HILFREICH UND GUT

Whoever he was, he died the year World War II began, six years into the Nazi time. He was born, as it happens—this is part of the outside reading—in the very border town where Hitler trumped up his provocation to invade Poland. And the text that the good Prof. Dr., or his family, chose to accompany him into eternity is from the great German national poet, Goethe, writing on "Das Göttliche": *the divine.* It's the poem's opening that gets quoted:

May man be noble,
Generous and good

Though I am momentarily distracted by the strange weightiness of the sculpted comma, I am soon struck by the fact that at least one immigrant to Berlin seems to have cleaved to the ideals of the Enlightenment, despite all provocations to the contrary.

But if I didn't find Gray's "Elegy" in this space, I wasn't necessarily after some twentieth-century equivalent—paradox?—either. Indeed, the names and the lifespans and the humble origins and the fancy titles and the texts, whether in Hebrew or German, though they filled my head with the imagination of a certain long-ago, didn't quite add up to the kind of awe that gripped me in Schönhauser Allee. What did it was the monuments themselves.

Orient yourself by following the perimeter of the graveyard triangle, where notable clans seem to have taken possession of a wall segment and mounted collective family memorials, including plaques or headstones where specific decedents were commemorated. Grandiose in conception, but now mostly in ruins; on my first circuit, the best I could do was to piece out from one classicizing gable the phrase *Awaken to eternal life*, which, though it's cited from the book of Daniel, sounds suspiciously Nazarene to me.

It's when you move toward the ample central spaces of the graveyard that you really see how much this tribe cared about honoring their dead. And spending money on it. Consider one roulette-wheel-shaped monument, so massive that it obliterates the rectilinear groundplan of the whole cemetery. At the hub a gigantic sandstone coffin shape, with the barely legible majuscule letters SELIGSOHN, topped by a pyramid, while the outer circle, thirty feet in diameter and festooned with six-pointed stars, leaves room for the naming of countless individual family members; history decreed that only four of them seem to have made it there (Figure 1.5). Compared with that act of assertion, a black granite tabernacle framed in three pilasters, a couple of zones to the west, might seem almost whimsical, were the pomp of the spectacle not underlined by the doubtless synthesized family name SENATOR. More immediately striking is the nearby pink marble wall of the STEINTHAL family, something between a fence and a fortification, including stumpy columns, trefoil medallions, and arches that look like windows in a slightly upscale tenement. And, taking a brief turn eastwards,

I'm sure that the GEIGER family were happy to throw considerable resources into their own capacious chunk of graveyard real estate, even though the arched construction framing the upper end of it looks suspiciously like an oversized headboard.

It's not just about money, though. These people had style. Or rather styles. Does the world contain any twelve acre parcel where one can traverse so much history of art? I like to begin with the forty foot wall of limestone honoring the apparently interlocking HERZ, KATZ, and GRAU families: there is something a little Egyptian about it, maybe because it reads as gigantic yet two-dimensional; and, to keep that sense of early history going, you can zip over to STETTINER, which looks like a festooned squashed pyramid. Then—we're marching through art history here—we glimpse FAMILY BOAS, who erected a tidy little granite Greek shrine to itself, but such architectural discretion wasn't enough for FRIEDHEIM, who structured their classical temple with Doric columns and pilasters, metopes and triglyphs.

At this point, I start losing track of classical vs. neoclassical, and begin to browse Romanesque. The stolid block of BENJAMIN LIEBERMANN, with tight little arches and short stout pillars, looks like something you'd see on the pilgrimage route if it crossed over into Cordoba. And who could resist the softly curvaceous inscription ADOLPH UND HENRIETTE BURCHARDT, densely adorned with faux Arabic?

Time for High Gothic, and, never mind the abyss that separates Bernard of Clairvaux or Abbot Suger from the Jews, this is one of the preferred styles for those in Schönhauser Allee who want to go all out. I like LION as much for their name as for their high medieval aedicule, which looks like a rose window without a cathedral behind it. And I appreciate the alternative afforded by JOACHIM LIEBERMANN, whose impressive Gothic share of the outside wall puts that rose window in its place by exchanging Notre Dame's delicate quadrants of tracery with a great big Jewish star. The Gothic goes about as far as it can go with REICHENHEIM, who composed a deep empty cathedral chapel in the shape of a bullet, framed by pedestals constructed of little granite gift boxes, the whole thing issuing in a continuous swirl of enclosure, where the actual deceased would be resting.

Let the dawn of the Renaissance be announced by GOLD-BERGER, who turns the ancient temple into an open-air space framed rhythmically by columns and pilasters; once again, I'm a sucker for the six-pointed star, here tucked with delicious syncretism between the volutes of Ionic capitals (Figure 1.6). Discretion, such as it is, goes out the window with HABERLAND. This open-air structure becomes a classical cryptoporticus, strewn in strategic places with palms and phoenixes, beetles and lizards, all doubtless bearing some sacred meaning. And what am I to say of DAVID KAPPEL? Small in size but packed with the whole glossary of Renaissance architectural classicism. Wreaths, scrolls, cornices, entablatures, friezes: neoclassicism abhors a vacuum.

This nineteenth-century living museum of the departed isn't all retro, however. Art nouveau offers up its vernacular generously. Some mortuary symbolism was doubtless understood at the intricate sight of stone made to represent the multiple folds of a cascading garment, whether its surplus of carving overlay an urn (SCHWABACH) or a catafalque (GINSBERG). And—just to prove how very stylish these consumers could be—some quite up-to-date looks are occasionally on view. PAUL MEYER transitions between the deliquescent romanticism of his elegantly broken column and the no-frills Weimar typography of the burial plaque itself; and there is even a higher level of hodgepodge in the blockish sarcophagi à deux of LEHMANN: on the one hand, stencil-style text, on the other hand, a busy decorative field of laurel, acanthus, oak leaves, and general nonrepresentational swags. Then, too, there are aggressively stark monuments—take note of LANDAU and BERTHOLD ISRAEL, both composed of huge square blocks and inscribed in rigorously unornamented lettering—whose 1930s appearance leaves one uncertain whether they were seeking *style moderne* or whether they recognized that a future quite beyond the reach of decor was closing in on them.

Make no mistake, though, the prevailing look of this tribe at its extravagant core was, even in death, joyously eclectic, however we may frame it in art history, or, more disturbingly, in history. What else could explain a Gothic-classical front-and-back wayside chapel like BODENSTEIN, complete with a Star of David hemorrhaging gold, surmounted by two pairs of stubby fingers miniaturizing the Ten Commandments, or HAMBURGER, which can only be described as a *Jugendstil* toilet?

Total disclosure obliges me to say that many of the monuments—and not only those from earlier and more orthodox epochs—are quite simple. There is, in fact, something like a standard gravestone model constructed of unadorned angular black granite; dozens of these bear not only an identifiably common style but also an identical signature: M. ZACHART. Clearly, a disciple of simplicity. But only for others, it seems. M. Zachart's own memorial, embracing wife and sister-in-law as well, while making use of what one takes to be the abundant family stock of granite, splays itself out in a grand array of cornices and gables, a class of embellishment denied to his many neighboring customers. Given such grandeur, and the fact that his name appears so often in Schönhauser Allee, can the personal inscription on his portion of the tomb—"His Works Follow after Him"—be anything but some sort of double-edged cemetery irony, considering how many of his works are stolidly present before us?

Why should all of this transport me to some kind of epiphanic Jew-state? Permit me, like some Zen master, to respond with a little story.

Solly, who didn't use to have two nickels to rub together, suddenly makes a killing in ladies' ready-to-wear. So he decides he needs high class art for his living room, and he goes to the number one gallery in town. The dealer shows him a thirty-foot painting with nothing but a field of white, plus one red dot in the middle. The price is $100K. "Are you kidding me?" says Solly. "It's just a dot!" After the dealer reassures him, Solly does some research and discovers it's the hottest thing going, so he buys it. Then Solly makes *another* killing. He decides he needs more art and goes back to the same dealer, who shows him the latest work of the same painter, only this time it has *two* red dots. "What do you think?" asks the dealer. "Should I wrap it up for you?" "Ehh," Solly answers, "*tsufil ongepotchket.*"

Translation of the Yiddish punch line (with, admittedly, much lost in the process): *too fussy, unnecessarily elaborate, overly deco-*

rated. Like many Jewish jokes, however terrible and creaky with endless repetitions, it offers an infinitely faceted glimpse into the culture that produced it. It's about money and whether it does or doesn't buy culture; it also assumes that the most important thing you do with money is to acquire culture. The *schmatte* magnate has no clue about culture, but he knows he wants it, and he knows where to acquire it. Once he forks over his money, he wastes no time at all to get on board with the concept of culture that he has literally bought into—so much that he becomes a sophisticated critic holding the line against anything that might pollute the culture he so expensively embraced while getting in on the ground floor.

But all that is just a prelude to the all-important concept of *ongepotchket*, because that condition of excess is the vanishing point of Jewish taste, the thing (to quote St. Augustine on God) whose center is everywhere and whose circumference is nowhere. Ornament defines culture—it's exactly what Solly is missing back in the sweat shops where he made the money in the first place—but the nouveau riche is terrified that he will pass across an invisible line into *too much* ornament, something, in fact, that he is all but inevitably bound to do. And the voice of the individual who is one step ahead, who landed on Ellis Island one boat earlier, so to speak, is always whispering in his ear the dreaded admonition: *tsufil ongepotchket*.

But before we consign Solly to the scrap heap of the incurably vulgar, let's take note of an undercurrent in the story. He may be a Philistine, either because he buys the first painting or because he doesn't buy the second painting. But huge white paintings with one red dot, or two red dots, are stupid (sorry, Robert Rauschenberg); they, and the people who spend big bucks on them, deserve each other. So Solly, bless his heart and whether he knows it or not, is exposing something very wrong with the culture that looks down upon him. And—this is my personal addition—what about Solly Jr.? He probably doesn't know bupkes about ladies' ready-to-wear (unless he's occasionally dressing in it, but we won't go there). Nevertheless, it paid for his education, and, growing up in that house—filled, one presumes, not only with the white painting but lots of other tchotchkes in varying states of *ongepotchket*—he may be in a position to take quite another stance on culture.

The Schönhauser Allee graveyard is the antidote to the white painting. The tribe who buried their dead here had entered a culture into which many of them were not born, but they had—again, many of them—made a great success of it. To be sure, they left other markers besides these tombs (we'll hear about some of those elsewhere in this book), but what we see in these twelve acres, sequestered from the city that granted them, with whatever restrictions, the rights of participation and citizenship, is a record of their lives. Beside the names, the dates, the birthplaces, the titles, and the poetry (terrible, but what else is new?), this is a thrilling field of *tsufil ongepotchket*. These Grecian temples and Gothic chapels, the experiments in Deco and Bauhaus, bear testimony to this community's collective refusal to listen to orthodoxies, whether of a Judaic sort (say, simple stone markers in the desert), or of the aesthetic sort (say, all-white paintings). In the process, these Sollys, and Solly Jr.'s, and Solly the Thirds created something beautiful, and, if this be kitsch, they made the most of it. When I stand amidst these monuments, in short, I go past elegy and through paradox onward to love.

Love begets labor. It's all very well to circulate in this space, anthropologically, with nothing but the stones themselves to teach me. But these are not the inhabitants of Samoa or the Trobriand Islands, any more than they are the anonymous villagers of Gray's "Elegy." These are the People of the Book, and they lived among the People of Minute Documentation. The archive, in short, is nearly infinite, and though my outside reading—such as I offered in connection with Prof. Dr. Heinrich Silbergleit—can barely lay claim on the depth with which they fashioned a culture, I must make an attempt to interlace a few strands, in the loosest of weaves, out of that dense original fabric, and in a haste that belies their long century of prominence.

Let us pull first on the thread of that same Heinrich Silbergleit (1858–1939). The statistician of everyday life in Berlin, he devised the simple expedient of buying rye bread at each bakery in the city, in order to determine a price curve; and from there he worked on the prices for fruits, vegetables, meat, and butter, pioneering the use of punch cards in standardizing the results. Moritz Meyer (1821–1883) was also a measurer, a physician who developed something called the "Meyer'sche Unterbrecher," which could calculate more precisely than ever before the tension in muscles and nerves.

What Meyer did was to harness the electricity of the body. In a related vein, Robert Remak (1815–1865), frustrated in an academic career despite the fact that ganglia were named after him, worked on the live current in the nervous system, the brain, and the spinal cord. And Peter Theophil Riess (1805–1883) crossed over between physics and medicine, pursuing the triboelectric effect, which explains why your cat's hair stands on end when you pet it.

Besides electricity, Remak and Riess had in common the friendship of Alexander von Humboldt, who failed to get the former a physician's place in the royal court at St. Petersburg but succeeded in gaining entrance for the latter into the Berlin Academy of Sciences. They were not alone in being on the receiving end of this enlightened patronage. Far from neurology and electrified cat hair, Michael Sachs (1808–1864), who hung around with the philosopher Schelling as well as von Humboldt, was a rabbi with a philological bent, famous for translating the Psalms and for delivering mesmerizing sermons.

Despite his up-to-date academic training, Sachs was a religious conservative. Not so Samuel Holdheim (1806–1860), whose radical claims urging limits on the secular power of rabbis earned him the title "Martin Luther of the Jewish faith." All of which was too much for Sachs, who tried to prevent him from being buried in Schönhauser Allee. The local authority was Rabbi Jacob Joseph Oettinger (1780–1860), himself an innovator. Years before, when he conducted the very first funeral on these grounds, he dared to preach in German, which earned him censure both from traditional Jews, who thought he was showing insufficient respect for the language of the Bible, and from the Prussian authorities, who thought he was taking assimilation too far. Whoever made the decision—and Oettinger was himself in the last year of his life—Holdheim was clearly admitted to the privileged circle. Four years later, Sachs ended up cheek by jowl with the enemy he would have banished.

Looking at the two of them together for eternity, it seems like a twist on the line about every town needing two synagogues, the one you attend and the one you wouldn't be caught dead in. Fortunately—if anything in a graveyard is fortunate—there are couples who cohabit better than Holdheim and Sachs. Simon Barthold (1827–1848) and Alexander Goldmann (1830–1848) were the two Jewish members of the *Märzgefallene*—the martyrs of March—who were killed on the barricades opposing the restrictions on liberty that were being enforced by the troops of Frederick William IV. They are interred in a single gracefully designed monument, their funeral oration given by the most towering of the figures in Jewish reform, Leopold Zunz (1794–1886), yet another innovator, whose eloquence as philosopher, writer, and educator earned him in his lifetime the title of Founder of the Science of Judaism.

Another kind of double grave—this one for husband and wife—for Hermann Makower (1830–1897; wife, Doris, 1840–1888), the liberal attorney who defended the great German historian Theodor Mommsen in Bismarck's action of slander against him and, after many rounds, gained an acquittal. And speaking of the Iron Chancellor brings us, a little jaggedly, to yet another couple joined in entombment. Ludwig Bamberger (1823–1899) went through the 1848 revolutions and earned himself a death sentence, itself evaded via exile and thence followed by amnesty and the founding of the Deutsche Bank. (Makower's client Mommsen referred to him, incidentally, as "the most German of all the Germans.") When his eventual gravemate, the liberal and sometimes radical legislator and jurist Eduard Lasker (1829–1884) died—in New York, of all places—Congress sent a message of condolence to the aforementioned chancellor, which proved no small embarrassment, since the decidedly illiberal Bismarck was hardly sitting shiva over this particular loss.

But things like shiva were up for grabs. For Israel Jacobson (1768–1828) the Mosaic faith meant steeple bells, organ, and the banishment of Hebrew, yarmulkes, and kosher laws; it also meant a political career, Jacobson having become for complicated fiduciary reasons a minor feudal lord and the personal agent of Jérôme Bonaparte in the secularization of certain Westphalian monasteries. In fact, the emancipatory politics of the midcentury gripped many of these liberalizing figures. Heinrich Bernard Oppenheim (1819–1880) moved in and among the radical fringes of revolutionary movements, sometimes as a journalist, sometimes as a would-be legislator, and occasionally as a Wiki leaks–style agent provocateur. No mere liberal, on the other hand, Joseph Stargardt (1821–1885): the year 1848 seems to have made him an anarchist. His cover was a highly successful bookstore near the Gendarmenmarkt, which was occasionally raided by the police in search of forbidden literature at the same time that it acted as a meeting place for the likes of (once again) Alexander von Humboldt. Bookseller and publisher Moritz Poppelauer (1824–1880) brought out editions of the Talmud; Julius Siegfried Joseephy (1792–1856), on the other hand, made his fortune—go figure!—publishing the Church Fathers.

Leopold Ullstein (1829–1899) sold more copies than Poppelauer or Joseephy. From the Talmud to the printshop is one sort of transition; Ullstein made a different career move, from the family business of selling paper wholesale to printing the news on those sheets of paper. His *Berliner Zeitung*—along with *Berliner Morgenpost*, it still exists today, though under different ownership—was sufficiently progressive (and sufficiently successful) that for a time the Emperor's soldiers were forbidden to buy it. Printed matter figured in another set of family fortunes, belonging to the Veits. The earlier generations began with cotton, dye, and banking; in later times Moritz Veit (1808–1864) ran something like the Poppelauer-Joseephy gamut in his publishing ventures, from the works of Michael Sachs and Leopold Zunz (just to mention some nearby cemetery neighbors) to those of Goethe, Schiller, and Fichte.

One of Moritz Veit's charitable projects was a Jewish Old People's home constructed on land immediately adjacent to the cemetery, whether as a gesture of warning or of comfort we cannot guess. Among the other supporters of the project was Jacob Israel (1823–1894), whose very traditional Jewish profession—retail—we have perhaps heard too little about. It gets even more stereotypical: Jacob's father Nathan peddled old clothes in the Scheunenviertel's Jüdenstraße; Jacob married upward (daughter of the chief rabbi of the British Empire), and opened a depart-

Gallery I

Figure 0.1, 0.2
The city-spanning M29
bus begins its route in
the urban cacophony of
Neukölln's Hermann-
platz; at the other
terminus, in Grunewald,
a tree-lined allée
invites passengers
into the countryside.
Photographs by Nick
Barberio.

Figure 0.3
Warm evenings along the Spree, with the Bode Museum as a backdrop, are the joyous scene for pizza, beer, and ballroom dancing; all ages and gender combinations are welcome. Photograph by Nick Barberio.

Figure 0.4
Even a humble copy shop in Berlin can occupy a nineteenth-century building whose exquisite decoration seems to have miraculously survived the city's devastation. Photograph by Nick Barberio.

Figure 0.5
At the appropriate season, hundreds of appropriately shaped huts spring up overnight along the streets and the transit hubs of Berlin; they dispense their delicious and perfectly photogenic strawberries for a few weeks and then disappear. Photograph by Nick Barberio.

Figure I.I, I.2
Pathways in the Schönhauser Allee cemetery may be elegantly manicured or covered in ivy and oblivion. Photographs by Nick Barberio.

Figure I.3, I.4
The passage of time and the erasures of identity exhibit considerable variety among the Schönhauser Allee gravestones. Photographs by Nick Barberio.

Figure I.5, I.6
The search for monumentality can be expressed via massive construction or via an elegant attempt to fuse the canonical forms of Greco-Roman architecture with the symbol of Judaism (*Seligsohn; Goldberger*). Photographs by Nick Barberio.

Figure 2.1
Jewish real estate developer Georg Haberland sits proudly at his desk, having inspired the creation of several Berlin neighborhoods, including the Bavarian Quarter, the Rheingau Quarter, and the Wagner Quarter. Courtesy of Corporate Archives Bilfinger Mannheim Germany.

Figure 2.2
Haberlandstraße in 1909. In the foreground, the building where the eponymous founder of
the neighborhood lived; in the background on the right, the residence of Albert Einstein and
his family.

Figure 2.3, 2.4
In the Bavarian Quarter luxuriant greenery envelops Regensburger Straße 30, whereas nothing intrudes upon the architectural lines of Viktoria Luise Platz 7 as it strives for the sky. Photographs by Nick Barberio.

Figure 2.5
Albert Einstein's former home in Haberlandstraße had become Berlin rubble by 1945, but one resident of the characterless structure that replaced it has claimed air rights for the theory of relativity. Photograph by Nick Barberio.

ment store, Kaufhaus N. Israel, right opposite Berlin's City Hall (slogan: "Israel ist reell"). They were sufficiently *reell* to shut their doors on *shabbos*, a step not taken by the myriad other Jewish department stores.

In a possibly related story, the N. Israel building housed a private synagogue, which was the domain of a vastly wealthy textile merchant named Louis Liebermann (1819–1894). Having cited names like Veit, Israel, and Liebermann, it becomes difficult to speak about individuals; better have recourse to terms like *clan* and *dynasty*. Each of them has its own history of upward, and typically westward, mobility, but the Liebermanns, whose remains occupy at least ten separate locations in Schönhauser Allee, are special. In fact, you can make a day of just visiting their various sites, comparing styles of headstone and gauging from the presence or absence of Hebrew just where they placed themselves in regard to tradition, or, alternatively, noting the network of intermarriage involving other such clans: Rathenau, Reichenheim, Hirschfeld, Marckwald.

But this group is also special because it includes one of Schönhauser Allee's biggest celebrities, the painter Max Liebermann (1847–1935): just look at the number of pebbles reverently placed on his obligingly flat memorial stone. Boosterism aside—and I confess to much rooting for the home team—he was indeed a great modernist painter, somewhere between classicism and impressionism, equally gifted in landscape, narrative, and portraiture. If only I could adequately translate his famous reaction to seeing the Nazis, fresh from their electoral victory, march through the Brandenburg Gate: (roughly) "I can't eat enough food to puke up as much as I'd like to." A Jewish joke, from the vintage year 1933.

A different kind of Jewish joke, or perhaps not a joke, on the memorial slab itself. This great artistic citizen of the world, master of European classicism and French impressionism, president of the Prussian Academy of the Arts, a proud citizen of Berlin, he painted portraits of some of his most famous (and least Jewish) fellow citizens, including Richard Strauss, Gerhart Hauptmann, and Paul von Hindenburg. At the top of the gravestone, before the Star of David, before "Max Liebermann," before the

German motto, itself taken from a biblical text as it appears in a Bach Cantata, in front of all of these there appears an inscription in the Hebrew alphabet, where he is named—not in German, not even in Hebrew, but in Yiddish: REB MOISHE LEEBERMAN. Such was the wholly unassimilated moniker with which he confronted eternity.

Speaking of tradition, the Burchardt clan had, like so many, Polish border origins, but before long Baruch Elias Burchardt (1797–1859) made money in oilcloth and went on to banking. Hermann Burchardt (1857–1908), however, couldn't wait to get out of the family business and go far afield; before being fatally ambushed by bandits in Yemen, he produced extraordinary photographs and drawings, among the earliest Western testimonies we have to the Middle East. He wasn't the only refugee from the ancestral business who traveled far afield. Paul Wilhelm Magnus (1844–1914), with a family fortune, again in textiles and banking, scoured the world for botanical samples and became a master mycologist. And botany was the escape as well for Nathanael Pringsheim (1823–1894), scion of Silesian industrialists, who abandoned medical school and devoted himself to studying plants under the microscope, discovering that algae had sex.

But on to more sedate sciences. Some family members rose *from* the pursuit of medicine, others rose *into* it. Heimann Wolff Berend (1809–1873) left yet another eastern town and his merchant family to become an orthopedic surgeon in Berlin, where he successfully performed the very first operation under anesthetic at the Charité Hospital. Max Rothmann (1868–1915), by contrast, was a second generation physician; he shuttled between his work on the central nervous system, his interest in setting up a primate lab on the island of Tenerife, and his efforts to help the World War I wounded. His eldest son got killed at the front, his second son was refused officer status and soon died as a common soldier. Whereupon Dr. Rothmann ended his own life, as is perhaps somehow communicated by the very rough hewn stone of his burial marker.

The tribe of Schönhauser Allee worked to make war as well as to heal its wounds. Many, as we have seen, began in textiles and expanded into larger financial enterprises. The arc of Ludwig Loewe (1837–1886) was more unusual. Fabric led his family to sewing machines; and sewing machines led to guns—both being precision instruments—which he ended up selling to armies all over the world (the guns, not the sewing machines). The undertaking was not without its perils: his younger brother, Isidor (1848–1910), had to file suit (successfully, in the end) against anti-Semites who claimed that the weapons, which got referred to as Jew Flints, were deliberately designed to explode in the hands of the soldiers who used them.

A less bellicose side of the family is evidenced in the tomb of Ludwig's wife, Sophie (1847–1876), who died young and is memorialized in a breathtakingly uncanonical portrait that appears on her quite unusual triangular monument. The only other instance of this practice in Schönhauser Allee is the memorial erected by Julius Model (1838–1920) for his son Paul (d. 1895). In both cases, it seems, inconsolable grief for untimely death occasioned the breaking of the second commandment. "Do not seek me here, | Seek me in your hearts," reads the Model inscription, perhaps suggesting that Julius is flaunting his disobedience of the injunction against graven images.

But back to war. Doctors and munitions makers are on the edges of the fighting itself, but then there is the case of Meno Burg (1789–1853). The long prohibition on Jews entering the Prussian officer corps was in some ways the very backbone of their social exclusion. Meno Burg fought it. Not only did he jump through decades of hoops, refusing, for instance, to convert, and finally attaining the rank of Major (Order of the Red Eagle, fourth class); he also exercised himself in print, having authored a technical manual with a twenty-nine word title that seems to boil down to something about architectural drawing.

Hermann Salingré (1833–1879)—he had fancied up his surname by reversing the last two letters and adding that rakish accent—brings together soldiering and writing in a different way, as a correspondent on the front lines of the Franco-Prussian War. At other times, he was variously the highly successful, and then quickly forgotten, author of more than a hundred stage comedies and the bankrupt former publisher of a newspaper. Physician Bernhard Wolff (1812–1879) did a lot better in the journalistic field. Owner of the *Berliner National-Zeitung*, he started assembling the latest information concerning business, stocks, and the economy, ending up as the forerunner of Dow Jones and the *Wall Street Journal*. Medicine seems to have been a flexible calling for others as well. In Silesia, Max Ring (1817–1901) treated wretchedly poor patients suffering from Hunger Typhus, while in Berlin he treated the upper bourgeoisie; on the side, he wrote stories, plays, and poems—several hundred, we're told—about all of these experiences. Like Salingré, he was prolific, successful, and, nowadays, largely forgotten, though he'll be remembered here, briefly, in chapter 3.

With titles such as *Five Cases of Diffuse Nephritis*, James Israel (1848–1926) was a different sort of doctor-author. Expert in tumor recognition (he had his own special "Israel'sche Palpation") and collaborator with Joseph Lister in the brand-new enterprise of operating room hygiene, he ended up creating an assembly line project of surgical intervention for sufferers from kidney disease all over Berlin. Israel may have developed his own eponymous palpation, but his *Doktorvater*, Ludwig Traube (1818–1876), far outdistanced him, what with (among others) Traube's Blockage, Traube's Pulse, Traube's Doubletone, Traube's Dyspnea, and the Traube-Hering-Mayer Waves.

One further eponym was his son, also Ludwig Traube (1861–1907), who followed the father in distinction, while veering away in profession. Ludwig Jr. became a philologist, one of the first scholars to take medieval Latin literature seriously and a fundamental theorist in the subject of textual transmission. And, speaking of transmission, if we move a generation back, we meet grandpa Traube (not buried here), who was—*nomen est omen*—a wine merchant. Both trade and name are captured in the exquisitely simple decoration on the tomb of the younger Ludwig—he died in his forties, of leukemia—which punningly represents a bunch of grapes.

Whether a younger generation working in the humanities represents a rise or a fall in dynastic fortune you might ask the Liebermanns. Max's younger brother, Felix (1851–1925), was sent to master the family businesses of textiles and banking in London and Manchester, but he stuck it out for a mere four years, whereupon he took his Britannic experience in quite another direction, becoming a widely published expert in twelfth-century English law.

Another branch of the Liebermann family veered out of commerce as well. Max's uncle Adolph von Liebermann (1829–1893) seems to have escaped textiles and banking even faster than his other nephew, medieval-minded Felix, but he moved in the direction of the arts. Adolph was, in short, an aesthete, not only with a good eye—he was, in fact, instrumental in recognizing Max's early talent and persuading the family to support it—but also, being a Liebermann, with a good purse. All of which enabled him to amass a great collection of German painting, and that in turn produced the kind of social connections with royalty that led to the Austrian emperor Franz Joseph ennobling him "for services to Prussian art"; hence that very un-Jewish *von*, and the imperial-style bier of his death monument. The art apparently didn't have to be German to excite royal interest. Markus Kappel (1839–1920) possessed a remarkable collection of Dutch and Flemish masterpieces. When Wilhelm II paid a respectful visit to Kappel's private gallery, one gossip sheet outed the event under the headline "The Kaiser's Newest Friend."

No difficulty in detecting that journalistic sneer, and yet imperial favor was not unknown among Schönhauser Allee denizens. Hermann Gerson (1813–1861), of humble origins (né Hirsch Gerson Levin) grew to be one of the most successful clothing manufacturers and retailers in the city, his career culminating in the commission to produce Kaiser Wilhelm I's coronation robe. The Manheimers (Moritz [1826–1916] and Bertha [1837–1918]) earned their wealth—a fortune that began with a winning lottery ticket, it should only happen to you—in the same trade. Upon the occasion of their diamond anniversary, the Emperor and Empress sent congratulations, probably less a recognition of dress-making than of the Manheimers' vast charitable enterprises, including their role as prime movers in that strategically situated Jewish Old People's Home.

One more good and faithful servant of imperial might: Louis Sussman-Hellborn (1828–1908), a versatile sculptor who worked in miniature forms and porcelain but also received the honor of producing a statue of Friedrich Wilhelm III for the ballroom of the same City Hall outside of which one could shop at Israel's Department Store (though never on Saturday). A more equivocal royal reception greeted the promising young playwright Michael Beer (1800–1833). Rapturously blurbed by Heine ("a fresh spring in that desert we call the German theater") and author of a drama about Indian pariahs, understood by everyone as an allegory for Jews, he was first encouraged but then ostracized by Bavarian king Ludwig II. When the young man was disinvited from leading the royal quadrille, he is said to have died of the shame.

Michael's elder and more famous brother was more in tune with his surroundings. Born Jakob Liebmann Meyer Beer but known to the world as Giacomo Meyerbeer (1791–1864), he is another of Schönhauser Allee's celebrities, though, as I discovered, his rather modest memorial stone is canted in such a way as to make the requisite pebble of remembrance almost impossible to lodge. More than anyone else and with the full magnificence of a triumphant career in Paris, Meyerbeer put the "grand" in "grand opera." It is a grim irony that in our time he is less famous for *Les Huguenots* and *L'Africaine* than for his vile treatment at the hands of Wagner; the ancestor of *that* irony is the fact that Meyerbeer was a great promoter of the youthful Wagner's music.

Quite possibly, neither Michael nor Giacomo would have been launched into their respective artistic careers were it not for another member of their family, Amalie Beer (1767–1854). This circumstance requires a parenthesis. It has not escaped the author's notice, nor will it the reader's, that this has been a catalogue of *men*. Easy to say that such a limitation is simply endemic to any piece of nineteenth-century history, but not entirely true. Where, one might ask, are the Mme de Staëls, the George Eliots, the Marie Curies, the Susan B. Anthonys of Schönhauser Allee? Is their absence merely statistical—that is, given the vast number of cemeteries and the tiny proportion of women who had professions in which even a modicum of fame was possible, were there not enough dead ladies to go around? Or is there some special oppression of women practiced by Jews, or by Berlin Jews, or by Schönhauser Allee Jews?

It gets worse, and it gets better. The good news—and we'll

hear about it elsewhere in this book—is that there was a very long tradition within the Jewish upper bourgeoisie of women who exercised cultural power by making their homes into meeting places for artists, politicians, and (even) royalty. The bad news, in a manner of speaking, is that in the case of the Beer/Meyerbeer clan, the powerful woman in question is (take a deep breath) a Jewish Mother in the prototypical sense. We're stuck, in short, between an oppression and a cliché.

Be all that as it may, Amalie, mother of Michael and Giacomo, was both a salonnière *and* a Jewish Mother. She came from great wealth—her father was said to be the richest Jew, or possibly richest man, in Berlin, until he lost one or both of those distinctions to her husband—and she turned her home into a meeting place for very boldface names indeed. No coincidence that music and theater, the interests of her two artistic sons, were the main focal points of her coveted invitations. Like all such promotional undertakings, it had its dangers: the portrait she commissioned of the eleven-year-old Giacomo as a musical prodigy, including subliminal Mozart references, was widely and (in my view) deservedly subjected to general derision.

Times change. Amalie Beer is enshrined in a multiple family tomb. Born sixty years later, Jenny Hirsch (1829–1902) gets a monument to herself, or almost to herself: hers is a curious design, looking something like an artwork resting on a Corinthian easel, with the very sober and traditional marker of her brother adjacent. If Beer lived in the age of salons, Hirsch lived in the age of treatises, one of the most important of which, J. S. Mill's *On the Subjection of Women*, she translated into German. On her own, she wrote both manifestoes and fiction, with, given the nature of the Zeitgeist, the liberal use of male pseudonyms.

No pseudonyms, however, in the work of Josephine Levy-Rathenau (1877–1921), another couple of generations later, who is memorialized without relatives or husband in evidence (in fact, she predeceased Max Levy, the distinguished physicist whom she married in 1900). Hirsch, coming from the poorest stratum of Jews, had focused her feminism on the problem of women's work; it's a tribute to Levy-Rathenau, whose wealthy family included a Weimar Foreign Minister (assassinated—but that's another story) and the head of the German Electricity Board, along with, by marriage, various Liebermanns, that she, too, understood employment to be a critical stage in the liberation of women.

Alas, the best-known woman in the graveyard, at least for a couple of decades, was more infamous than illustrious. It is almost impossible to disentangle the strands of scandal involving Dorothee Croner (dates unknown; her given name is missing from the substantial monument, but it is highly probable that this was indeed her family's tomb). A divorce; possible adultery; sexual accusations; a history of alleged blackmail attempts and police investigations of them; claims that there were, or weren't, pay-offs; affidavits that there were signed statements that no one ever saw; sleazy third party involvements on Croner's behalf, which, once Croner abandoned the legal actions, continued to be pursued by the sleazy third party/accomplice himself.

The fact that the co-star in this scandal was Gerson von Bleichröder (1822–1893) and that this central figure in Bismarck's Germany, the Iron Chancellor's most powerful financial and political supporter, should live for decades under a cloud of suspicion, some of it quite possibly justified, concerning adultery, perjury, and perversion of justice, can act as a kind of antidote to the threads of self-congratulation that our tour through this cemetery engenders. Does a Jew-on-Jew scandal betoken a gruesome coming of age of this community, as they move from being rag peddlers to retailers to surgeons to art historians to—what?— *National Enquirer* headlines? Or does it add up, as of course it *did*, to just another occasion for widespread anti-Semitism? One salient detail: Croner was brazen enough at one point to sue in court for nonpayment of blackmail; the disbursement in question, beside involving 90 Reichsmarks per month, included a bonus of 75 Reichsmarks payable on each of four High Holidays. Only within the community of Schönhauser Allee would that lucrative bit of Jewish extortion have been possible.

One more joke upon these two entangled unfortunates. In the (unlikely) event that you have threaded the labyrinth of this burial ground in the order in which I have presented these forty or fifty inhabitants—an order by no means chosen for its convenience as a pedestrian itinerary—you'll now discover that the graceful Bleichröder monument, with its arches and pilasters, topped with a lavish baroque urn, finds itself immediately adjacent to the imposing granite block that bears the name of his bitterest enemy. In fact, you will scarcely be able to read the inscription GERSON VON BLEICHRÖDER without the lapidary letters CRONER pressing themselves into your field of vision.

And, now that I have taken you back from history into the geography of the cemetery itself, I should add that if you stand in the position where you have this ominous double sight, you are a very few feet from where our slackly woven chronicle began. If you choose this moment to review Prof. Dr. Silbergleit, you'll notice, besides Goethe's solemn lines about man's nobility, an accession number: 22744, which, since he was one of the last to be interred here, gives us something like a rough count on the graveyard's total population. (You're also not far from Sara Meyer, whose headstone sports the epochal "1" of this century-long history.) That five-digit figure reminds me how many more stories I might have told—of Joseph Pitsch, the master plumber with (fittingly?) a tomb made of metal; of Julius Lessing, who brought Berlin's great Museum of Decorative Arts into being; of Lazarus Bendavid, the Kantian Bible critic; of Rudolph Arnhold the Coal King and Joseph Jacob Flatau the Hops King. But 22744 summons other thoughts as well. If we cannot rid ourselves of horror at the idea of numbers *on* Jews and numbers *of* Jews, it may be worthwhile, as we look at Statistician Silbergleit and some of the 22,743 around him, to recall that these magnificent twelve acres signal something more than deaths. Publishers and pipe-fitters, kidney surgeons and feminists, travelers to Tenerife and Yemen, purveyors of sewing machines and medieval Latin: these individuals, one by one, may not have left grand records of themselves, but together they offer an impression of what it meant for a century that Berlin was enriched by Jewish lives.

2

Places: Bayerisches Viertel

Speaking of lives rather than deaths, we turn now from a graveyard to a housing project. Earlier, I offered these two locations
in terms of contraries: nineteenth vs. twentieth century, east
vs. west, dwelling place vs. resting place. But there is one more
opposition that may prove even more significant. The cemetery
in Schönhauser Allee was, by its very nature, *restricted*, to use
the midcentury code word for the exclusion of an alien religious
group: think Gregory Peck in *Gentleman's Agreement* changing his
name from Green to Greenberg in order to ferret out the anti-
Semites of Darien. In reverse, of course. To be buried in those
twelve acres, one had to be a (literally) dues-paying member of
the Jewish Community.

The Bayerisches Viertel, on the other hand, was *integrated*,
to use yet another code word with a slightly jagged pattern of
association. How integrated was it, exactly? Appropriate that we
closed the last chapter with the question of numbers and the
person of Silbergleit the statistician. In fact, it's quite difficult to
nail down the numbers for the Jewish population in individual
Berlin neighborhoods as of, say, 1930. The most reliable claims
seem to be proportional: 4% of the city's population was Jewish,
we're told; and Schöneberg, the district inside which the Bavarian Quarter finds itself, seems to have had something approaching double that density of Jewish inhabitants. So maybe one person out of twelve was a Jew, probably higher within the Bavarian
Quarter itself. Not in any case a gigantic statistical presence. But
it's interesting to play with comparables. In a 2010 census of US
Jewish population, the highest proportion by state is 8.3%—New
York, so what else is new?—while the lowest is South Dakota
at, and I quote, "0.0%." Leaving aside the disturbing revelation
that Mount Rushmore is *Judenfrei* (apparently not quite: Google
informs me that there are shuls in Sioux Falls, Rapid City, and

Aberdeen), we need to remind ourselves that even the largest of these numbers is pretty small. The same, doubtless, goes for many minorities: Jews are not alone among those groups that make far more noise, or have far more noise made *about* them, than their numbers suggest. But those are phenomena to be analyzed in a different kind of book.

We've got, then, a Berlin neighborhood where the proportion of Jews in 1930 was about the same as that on Staten Island today. No one gets on the Ferry at Battery Park to look for bialys or Borscht Belt comedians, and yet the Bavarian Quarter, back in the day, was so Jew-identified that it was widely known as *Die Jüdische Schweiz*. That nickname itself has long stopped me in my tracks. Bracketing for the moment the *Jewish* part, why *Switzerland*? Certainly not because Switzerland itself has the relevant ethnic associations (proportion of Jewish population: 0.23%); nor does it reference any supposed special safety across the Alps, since the term predates the flight of Jews from Germany. Neutrality? Peace? Industriousness? Cheese with holes? It can't be along the lines of the immortal Graham Greene line, "In Italy for 30 years under the Borgias they had warfare, terror, murder, and bloodshed, but they produced Michelangelo, Leonardo da Vinci, and the Renaissance. In Switzerland they had brotherly love, they had 500 years of democracy and peace, and what did that produce? The cuckoo clock." Quite the contrary, one would have thought.

Be that as it may, a stretch of Berlin where at least 90% of the population is certifiably gentile is, virtually from the start, understood as a neighborhood defined by Jews. And in these pages I am giving it quintessential status as a twentieth-century embodiment of what it means to me to be a Jew. How come?

There is an easy, if partial, answer, and it relates to the very origins of the place. The Bayerisches Viertel was, in fact, the brain child of a Berlin Jew (Figure 2.1). We paused briefly in the previous chapter over an ornate classicizing burial monument, with a mixture of antique, Judaic, and untraceable symbolic signs, containing the remains of Salomon and Olga Haberland, who died in 1914 and 1925 respectively. Although there was plenty of room in that complex for other Haberlands—and such family groupings were the norm among the more grandiose of Schönhauser Allee shrines—in this case the eldest son and his wife provided themselves with a quite different monument, also classicizing, but in a radically divergent way. The younger Haberlands are memorialized in an exquisitely dainty round temple, which they share with a couple named Bernhardt and Betty Gutmann. It's not apparent what kinship these individuals share, but, as it turns out, the whole *mishpocheh* can tell us something about the origins of the Bayerisches Viertel.

Haberland père, whose mercantile operations go back to the classic evolution from textiles to banking, became the principal figure in a major Berlin real estate operation in 1890, taking on as major partner the Dresdner Bank, whose chairman of the board was one Eugen Gutmann. What the relations among the various Gutmanns may be is unclear, the more so since Eugen's entire immediate family converted and is buried in a Protestant cemetery. What is certain, however, is the prodigious developments that took place in the next generation. The son, Georg, was nothing short of an urban genius—a Robert Moses, let's say, with a more articulated vision of the modern metropolis (considering that he published dozens of books in urbanology), and a lot more money of his own. Textiles had begotten banking, which begot real estate; then real estate begot construction companies, which in turn begot striking changes in the city. There are many ways to describe these circles within circles. We could refer to it as the kind of totalizing monopoly that derives from land-owning, money-lending, the control of the construction industry, and the power conferred when special rights are granted by municipal authorities. Or we could call it a Jewish conspiracy.

But let us step back from that precipice and take note of the residential real estate scene as Berlin enters the twentieth century. At that moment, the proverbially rising middle class is aggressively westward bound, on the move from the densely packed noisy and gritty parts of the city (like the Scheunenviertel), where industry and commerce exist cheek by jowl with crowded living conditions. Suburbs—soon to become parts of the city themselves—like Charlottenburg, Wilmersdorf, and

Schöneberg beckon, and there is an energetic competition to attract those residents capable of bringing value with them.

At which point, Georg Haberland starts inventing neighborhoods from scratch. Economically speaking, it's a carefully articulated vision. The super-rich are building private villas farther west in still bucolic precincts like Grunewald (our destination, you may recall, on the M29 bus); the lower classes remain in the center and east. Haberland goes after the upper middle, and he builds his vision of the comfortable urban surroundings that they will pay for. But as with the work of many such individuals, the projects are as much about culture as about economics. If, today, you were to go to a couple of other western parts of the city—and I urge you to do so—you might, in one case, hang a left from Isoldestraße into Brünnhildestraße, or, in another, discover that all the streets (e.g., Rüdesheimer Platz, Marcobrunner Straße) had names taken from towns in the far west of Germany. It's all Georg Haberland's doing. He decided that one of his new neighborhoods should honor Wagner and another the Rhineland.

But his first and grandest invention was the neighborhood that honored Bavaria. Not the Bavaria of a big city like Munich but rather a semi-imaginary landscape of quaint towns unspoiled since medieval times. To be sure, the city-planning itself did not represent anything bucolic or medieval. The grid of vertical and horizontal overlaid with diagonals that meet in multi-sided monumental plazas has more to do with Haussmann's Paris or L'Enfant's Washington than with Berchtesgaden. What does, however, nail down the Bavarian imagery is the domestic architecture itself. Tall, narrow structures with a combination of turrets and mansard roofs were clearly meant to evoke the building stock that could be found back in the towns memorialized in the expressly minted street names. And, since the indigenous avatars of these apartment houses were likely to have been public buildings rather than dwelling places, the whole ensemble is built on a jagged repurposing of architecture and the lives lived inside it.

Such repurposing should come as no surprise because the

whole Bavarian Quarter was born, after all, as a fantasy. At a moment around 1900, in a city that found itself playing on a world stage even though it was centuries younger than other such cities, the possibility of radical urban creation ex nihilo was joined with a capitalism of interlocking directorates that empowered a newly moneyed class, consisting notably of Jews, or Jews-until-recently. The parallel that springs to mind from our own national experience is none other than Hollywood. A new territory inside a new country, whose creations were—in this case, literally—fantasies. I think of my distant cousin, Samuel G. Engel, who spoke nothing but Yiddish until he started school but ended up at 20th Century Fox, president of the Screen Producers Guild, and producer of movies like *My Darling Clementine*, which claimed to offer the official account of the shootout at the O.K. Corral. (Or, as my mother, unimpressed after a private screening, renamed it, "The Oy Vey Corral.") There are lots of more famous instances throughout the arts, of course: Aaron Copland, who taught us what a rodeo should sound like; Rodgers and Hammerstein, who more or less invented the state of Oklahoma; Irving Berlin, who invoked God's special blessing on America; and then there's the very first shot in the most classic American movie of all, picturing a huge placard declaring that *Gone with the Wind* is A DAVID O. SELZNICK PRODUCTION. You might as well say that of the Civil War itself, in twentieth-century filmic consciousness: A DAVID O. SELZNICK PRODUCTION.

Haberland's transplantations into newly expanding Berlin, whether referencing Rhineland towns, Wagner's operas, or Bavarian villages, sought to lay claim on something quintessentially German, something by no means native to his own background, nor, for that matter, to the cosmopolitan city in which he was constructing these castles in the air. But if Haberland is turning a fantasy into bricks and mortar and then putting it on the market, Germanness is not the only commodity up for sale. In fact, he was riding an international wave. Before the late nineteenth century, the truly moneyed classes, if they lived in the city at all, had private townhouses. As more citizens were entering into wealth and—this is particularly important from a Jewish perspective—identifying themselves as fundamentally urban rather than as rooted in some ancestral stretch of countryside, capitalism obliged by inventing luxury multiple housing.

For which I am very grateful to capitalism. I grew up in multiple dwelling Manhattan, of the humble sort—not exactly the Dakota or the Beresford or 1185 Park Avenue, epically celebrated as the titular subject of a fetchingly written memoir, but just enough on the edge of that culture so that I could peer *into*, and occasionally *out from*, those windows. The experience has framed my life in apartment house structures. We lived in an "M" apartment. The "L" and the "N," though next door to us, were understood to be, in some existential sense, *different*, though once, when I visited an "N," I discovered—in some infantile experience of the *unheimlich*—that it was the exact mirror image of our "M." The vertical mattered in its own way as much as the horizontal, yet, though it seemed to promise sameness, I remember discovering during an episode of Halloween trick-or-treat (which I found harrowing, but that's another story) that at the very top of my childhood building the familiar "M" designated a space of quite different shape. The whole thing has left me with a set of fascinations based on the shape of apartment buildings: vertical sameness, horizontal difference, symmetry, asymmetry, conformity, non-conformity, and (this will be particularly important in the Bavarian Quarter) the struggle for access to outside light, given that these dwellings, however sumptuous, are generally deprived of that complete set of north, east, south, and west exposures that even the humblest detached hovel enjoys.

In practice, all this means that I love to stare at outsides and imagine the insides that they enclose. But what is for me enduring voyeurism was, a century or so ago, the realizable fantasy of living large for some upwardly mobile Berliners. Haberland knew what his people were looking for. On the one hand, he was able to imitate traditional free-standing dwellings by offering lavish ten-room layouts with expansive dimensions and high ceilings, including music rooms, conservatories, balconies, and adequate space for servants. On the other hand, recent technological progress was such that these new constructions could offer modern conveniences—electric lights, automatic hot water heating, even central vacuum cleaning installations (go figure!)—that those ancestral townhouses were struggling to retrofit.

Of course, neither you (dear reader) nor I are likely to spend much time inside these grand establishments, let alone live in them, so our situation is pretty much like my childhood position imagining what the spaces and lives were like in apartments beyond the confines of 14M (which was really 13M, but that's another story). Which is perfect, because the *Altbau* structures of the Bavarian Quarter turn out to be infinitely more suggestive from this outside-looking-in perspective than the taller and remoter apartment houses of my New York youth. Again, though, it's those fascinating coordinates of same and different that will anchor the experience of the urban walk.

It is, after all, perfect strolling territory, for which we have the authority of the man who taught Walter Benjamin what it meant to be a *flâneur*, Franz Hessel (in return, Benjamin referred to him in print as "a Berlin peasant"), who himself resided within the Viertel at Lindauer Straße 8. His writings take him all over the city, but near the end of his little book, *Spazieren in Berlin*, he celebrates his home turf:

> The Bavarian Quarter is not laid out in so rectangular and straightforward a way as most of Berlin West. And instead of enjoying that, we thankless souls curse the fact that we constantly get lost in all this Heilbronn, Regensburg, Landshut and Aschaffenburg. And it can't be made straight. . . . But we shouldn't be too stern with the Bavarian Quarter. When it was built, the world wasn't yet arranged on that great flat universal conveyor belt where we now live.

As armchair *flâneurs*, we can afford to step off the world's conveyor belt ourselves.

Let's plant ourselves, then, in front of a couple of Bavarian Quarter apartment buildings. Bozener Straße 4 and 5, neither the humblest nor the grandest of these residences, can stand as archetype. The base pattern is a given: ground floor plus four upper stories and an attic, each level divided into two apartments. The front door, marked by eye-catching architectural ornament, anchors the structure in dead center. With this focal point securing a central core from entryway to the fifth floor gable, the rest of the building is free to express, and to complicate, the play of symmetry.

Bozener Straße 5 stands almost completely passive before this task: perfectly rectangular bays, gently curving balconies, attic window treatments scrupulously left-right identical. Bozener Straße 4, on the other hand, exhibits a riot of variation. On one side, the balconies are rectangular and excavated within the building's outer shell; on the other side, they are shallow semicircles that project forward from it. At the ground level, where outward extension isn't practical, a different play of asymmetry is invented, by which the left and right sides, one with a balcony and the other without, are unified by a curving arch rather than a square shape—a pattern replicated, with other variations, three stories upward. And the ornamentation here is similarly varied: decorative rectangles appear in a sequence where vertical and horizontal play off against same and different, a pattern further complicated in the building's central core, where curvature gets introduced into the rectangle.

Admittedly, these are variants that only a connoisseur would find interesting, or indeed notice. But a well-guided promenade through the neighborhood introduces radical deviations in the system. Before even leaving Bozener Straße, consider color. You need only follow the intriguing palette of Nos. 3, 11/12, and 17— rose, café au lait, ochre—to start noticing vast differences in design. The first implodes the balconies in the center and stages them in four distinct architectural orders that proceed from ground floor upwards. The second renounces the conventional balcony in favor of interior bays but compensates with little inset side terraces anchored in a Doric column. The third, which possesses the privilege of a corner lot, seizes this advantage with unusual modesty, marking the pivot in a sequence of tiny triangular window-parapets.

But let's venture farther. And where else but toward Haberland himself—his own building located in his eponymous street (Figure 2.2). (The interlinear on that subject is that he intended the nomenclature to honor his father, whose name, of course, he

light is just right, and you put yourself in a certain sweet spot, at the end of Regensburger Straße right below those anthropomorphic gangsta columns, No. 7, for all its monumentality, becomes almost transparent, as you catch the blue sky through the building and beyond, following the sight lines into one side of the tower's interior and out the other; you'll feel you almost know what it would be like to live there.

Now, I can't make the claim that I *have* lived there, but, courtesy of an obliging friend, I have spent one afternoon inside a genuine Viktoria-Luise-Platz dwelling. No surprise in the sunbathed magnificence of the front rooms, adorned with countless linear feet of a Roman-style Renaissance frieze, whose elements—windmills, clipper ships, body-building cherubs, a giant squid—eluded my training in iconography. But the real discovery, the solution to that apartment-house problem of failure to access 360° of light, lay behind. It turns out that all the windowless depth which gets renounced in the design of the front rooms contributes instead to a completely different kind of space, so characteristic of the city's architecture that it is known as the Berliner Zimmer. Halfway back in the building, a deep, almost cavernous room occupies the full breadth of the house, with one single window's worth of external access, and that fronting on an alleyway. Far from being a detriment in the life of these grand abodes, the Berliner Zimmer became their hub. This was the place where the occupants were most at home, where they dined and chatted and played music or cards, and where, sheltered from the public space of the front rooms, so copiously endowed with access to the outside world, these prosperous citizens lived their lives en famille. The Berliner Zimmer—the thought occurs to me, disturbingly—was the ancestor of that bourgeois invention of suburban America, the Family Room.

So, with this peek into the inner sanctum of a Bavarian Quarter domicile, we have caught sight of where the Jews, or a fortunate few of them, lived. And who were the Jews who lived there? Oddly enough, we have a very precise way of knowing. But this will take us away from neighborhoods and buildings and lead us rather into a book or, more precisely, an annual volume that went through two editions before the project was abandoned. Outside of those who are hunting up Jewish genealogies, the undertaking is not very well known. And since, like many reference works, it has mostly been utilized simply for the information that could be squeezed out of it, I'm not sure anyone has recognized just how bizarre an undertaking it actually was.

Permit me to explain via an admittedly imprecise analogy. Let us shift, a bit recklessly, from one minority group to another, and allow me to imagine it in my own present-day time and place. This group's numbers are fairly robust, especially in urban areas, including many prosperous individuals, and it has attained a reasonable degree of acceptance among the majority, though pockets of prejudice remain. Some members like to stick to their own kind, whereas others are more open to fraternizing with the majority. However they may feel about intermingling, many in the group would be happy for more information as to who the members of their own group actually are. So a few of them get together and publish something called *The Homosexual Address Book of Greater New York*, and alongside introductory material about gay organizations and biographies of prominent figures in the community, the bulk of the volume consists of 75,000 names and addresses of homosexuals in the five boroughs, listed in alphabetical order. By flipping through its pages you can precisely locate the residences of, say, Anderson Cooper, Stephen Sondheim, and Martina Navratilova, not to mention checking up on that eleventh grade music teacher of yours whom you've been wondering about.

This is, of course, a fantasy, *Gott sei Dank*. But I think it begins to convey the sheer oddity of *Das Jüdische Adreßbuch für Groß-Berlin*, which appeared in 1929 and again in 1930. There is another, perhaps more reliable indicator of something edgy about the project, even in its own time. This book, despite all the specificity involved in its thousands of names and addresses, as well as a hundred pages of material about the Jewish community and sixty pages of advertisements for everything from typewriters to exterminators, is completely silent as to the persons or entities responsible for it. Even today, the editor or publisher of the *Jewish Address Book* remains unidentified, and the imprint (Goedega-Verlags Gesellschaft Berlin) appears nowhere else but on these two volumes' title pages.

All of which makes it especially interesting to decode the language of the prefaces to the two editions, both anonymously undersigned only "Editorial Office and Publishing House of the Jewish Address Book for Greater Berlin." From the start the tone is defensive. Merely the news that a *Jewish Address Book* was in the planning stages, we're told, produced, along with much enthusiasm, certain "repercussions," or even "opposition." To which the (anonymous) undersigned responds with a barrage of arguments. Against the naysayers it is asserted that their hostility arises from a politics that favors total Jewish assimilation, even erasure—hence their distaste for public group identification qua Jews—and that this is by no means a desirable goal. (It's apparent, though, that the project steers clear of any ultraorthodox, anti-assimilationist strands within the community as well.) And, as regards those who object because they hope to conceal the fact that they are Jewish, these motives are "unworthy," "senseless," and "foolish." On the positive side, the preface cites the fact that, owing in part to the displacements of persons at the end of the World War, the Berlin Jewish population has soared (the figure given is 200,000 "souls"), and, despite the robustness of the community, the Jews are lacking a force that can bind them together. "This work," the preface announces, "seeks to create a spiritual center."

Eighteen months later, in June of 1931, the attacks—but also the defenses—appear to be more aggressive, and the whole thing is presented with a certain amount of denial. On the one hand, "political and economic woes cloud the horizon"; on the other hand, "the past year has demonstrated that we overestimated the extent of opposition to the project." Despite this claim of minimal resistance over the previous year, a newly intricate defense of the enterprise is mounted. Whenever there are acts of political violence, for instance when a certain Schlesinger blew up a railway train, the popular press blames it on the Jews; now, the Preface proudly argues, everyone will know who is and who isn't a Jew. The bomb-toting Schlesinger, we're told, wasn't a Jew, "never had been, and only happened to possess a surname in common with some Jews." "Our work," this second preface intones, "has nothing to do with any political or even religiopolitical considerations." The address book exists for practical purposes only, merely to clarify "who is a Jew and who is not a Jew." And it expresses confidence that it will build new bridges between the Jewish and non-Jewish communities. The only flaw that it freely acknowledges is that the previous edition did not do its research fully enough to include *all* who qualified. Indeed, we're told that the editors received more complaints from people who were disappointed at *not* being included in the directory than from those who objected to finding their names on the list. *Really?*

Whatever the truth of these proud assertions, and however cruelly mocked they are by subsequent history, the *Jewish Address Book*, in addition to providing us with extraordinary demographic data, paints a unique picture of a certain historical moment that was as proud as it was fragile. The intricate footwork performed here between separatist and assimilationist impulses will come as no surprise—it operates, after all, even in the most benignly placed of minority communities where no nightmare history can reasonably be contemplated—but the sheer fact of the 75,000 names (again, numbers *of* Jews, numbers *on* Jews) must set this project apart from anything that the world has seen before or since. In its own way, it is a monument to Jewish Berlin as impressive as the Bavarian Quarter itself.

It's not the monument of the *Jewish Address Book* that principally concerns us here, however, but all its painstakingly harvested information. We've walked the streets of the Bavarian Quarter and taken note of some remarkable dwellings; now, let's fill in some names. For which exercise another astonishing archival object comes into view. It is possible, merely sitting at one's computer, to locate the register of all Berlin residents, year by year, going as far back as 1799 and as far forward as 1943. Indeed, one can move street by street, house by house, through every neighborhood. And since the *Berlin Address Book* offers slightly more information than the *Jewish Address Book*, by cross-referencing these two projects of almost maniacal surveillance—again, we observe a pair of overlapping cultures with a similar devotion to record keeping—we learn not only the names of the Bavarian Quarter's inhabitants but also gain a few more bits of intelligence about them.

We can determine, for instance, that that jauntily adorned Regensburger Straße building housed a Felix Löwinsohn and a Hella Vogel; he owned commercial agencies, she—whose maiden name, we learn, was Roth—was retired. He, it turns out, lived on the floor decorated with the sculpted monkey in the tree, and she on the floor with the male and female columns. Our two paradigm structures at Bozener Straße 4 and 5 housed three merchants and a sales representative (Messrs. Rubinstein, Behrendt, Levy, and Ledermann, respectively); their phone numbers are also available, should you be interested. Perhaps it's no surprise that the inhabitants of the magnificent pink classical edifice at Hewaldstraße 9 get identified with slightly loftier occupations. Frau Kuschnitzsky on the second floor was the widow of an investor, the brothers Gustav and Markus Goldmann on the third floor were engineers, and Robert Robitschek, who lived in the plein air environment of the top story, was a banker.

In a similar vein, we can sniff something of the upper crust among the Viktoria-Luise-Platz inhabitants. Alfred Bergmann, at No. 7, the grandest of buildings on the square—he lived on the first floor (European style, often called the *belle étage*) and therefore, alas, not in the see-through turret—was a "Direktor" (presumably the head of a company), while his neighbor on the ground floor, Berta Wasbutski (née Sperling), was the widow of a medical consultant; that was the occupation as well of Dr. Eugen Fischer, who lived in fortress-like No. 12A, alongside Dr. Leo Selbiger, attorney and notary. And Arno Siegfeld, a wholesale dealer in iron, occupied not one but two Viktoria-Luise-Platz buildings, his business on the third floor of No. 4, and his residence on the second floor of No. 12—which means, incidentally, that he may have lived in the very apartment, with its squid reliefs and comfy Berliner Zimmer, that I was given the privilege of visiting.

Perhaps it seems as though we've schlepped our way through the whole Bavarian Quarter just so I could describe a few pretty buildings and pinpoint the whereabouts of a scrap iron dealer. In fact, though, I love the very ordinariness of these inhabitants' resumés, the fact that a bunch of commercial functionaries— would it help if I added Jenny Wachsmann the language teacher and Richard Kaufmann the wine merchant, in 2 and 4 Hewaldstraße, respectively?—made their homes in such lovely surroundings.

I also love the fact, and the institutions, of their collective community.

One of the earliest of these collectives remains vigorously in effect today, and, for the price of a couple of euros, you can still take full advantage of it. Within a few years of the neighborhood's inception, the city of Schöneberg (as it then was) committed itself to Germany's first ever publicly financed subway line. And the U4 remains a quite distinctive gem in the vast Berlin transport system. The visionary makers of this mini-railway hooked a mere four stations on to the larger network at Nollendorf Platz, each of them a simple little jewel box of early twentieth-century design. Viktoria-Luise-Platz is the first stop, but I suggest as well a detour via Rathaus Schöneberg—the prettiest U-Bahn station in Berlin, according to some—where the outdoor view is of lovely Rudolf Wilde Park. Yet it isn't so much the touristical charms of the U4 that tell the most important story. Rather it is the fact that they were designed to be a little bit closer together than in the previously constructed stretches of the city's U-Bahn system. It seems as though those same civic authorities, stretching back to Georg Haberland, who wanted to provide the residents of this little urban utopia with electric light and automatic vacuum cleaning, went to considerable expense so that no one had to walk more than a few hundred yards to arrive at a train that would whisk them to center city.

Granted, erecting a little train line that enables a set of lawyers and company directors to abbreviate the pedestrian portion of their commute is not everyone's idea of the ultimate civic mitzvah. In fact, though, the Bavarian Quarter turns out to have been the birthplace of some highly significant institutions devoted to social progress, some of which, like the U4, can still be observed.

Should you, in fact, follow my advice and take a stroll around the Rathaus Schöneberg station, you will come face-to-face with a lovely little labyrinth of domestic architecture that occupies the square block northwest of the corner of Badensche Straße and Martin-Luther Straße. If you explore the whorls of its open and closed courtyards, you'll find that it is on a more massive scale and more consistently designed than the sorts of structures around, say, Viktoria-Luise-Platz. And there is a good reason for that. Built in 1906–1907, this was one of the first experiments in cooperative housing, specifically designed for government workers. The Beamten-Wohnungs-Verein was the debut work of a young Jewish architect, Paul Mebes, who not only designed similar cooperative dwelling projects throughout Berlin but also pioneered a notable progression from the retro style of the Bavarian Quarter toward unmistakable traits of the New Objectivity, Bauhaus, and modernism.

Indeed, if you're willing to tear yourself away from the Bavarian Quarter toward some outer Berlin neighborhoods, including Pankow, Lichtenberg, and Wedding, you can pursue a whole timeline in the modernization of urban domestic architecture through the work of Mebes and his collaborator and brother-in-law, Paul Emmerich. It's no coincidence that innovation in style—for instance, striking new ways in which extensively repeated building elements, like windows or staircases, can turn beautiful rather than monotonous—should so closely accompany the enterprise of cooperatives erected for the purpose of housing an expanding urban population. In one sense, it's quite the opposite of Haberland's elite multiple mansions inside Bavarian castles. But in another sense, as one can see by pursuing the work of Mebes and Emmerich, it is precisely the social gospel of a neighborhood like the Bavarian Quarter that allows for translation into a set of styles that helped to redefine mass housing and, in the process, modernity itself: call it utopia trickledown.

Education in a modern vein was also a priority in the Bavarian Quarter, and here, too, it is interesting to observe the interplay between philosophy and the buildings in which the philosophy was practiced. The Werner-Siemens-Realgymnasium was famous for its liberal approach to pedagogy and notable for its high proportion of Jewish students. Ironically, though, it was housed in the most bombastic of faux medieval castles, whose twin silo-like towers, on the corner of Hohenstaufen and Münchener Straßen, even today loom high atop most of the neighborhood's roofs.

Quite a different story—and, alas, without any surviving architecture—was the vastly influential art school founded by Albert and Klara Reimann. Originating in 1902 as a small, private, Jewish-oriented Sunday art school, the enterprise took on its own life in transforming the principles of movements like Arts and Crafts and Secession into a whole range of graphic work oriented in a radically new fashion toward the marketplace. In 1931, when the Reimanns erected a stunningly theatrical home for their school in the heart of the Bavarian Quarter, the façade trumpeted in majuscule the range of graphic work that could be studied inside—PAINTING | SCULPTURE | INTERIOR DESIGN | ADVERTISING | TEXTILE DESIGN | FILM | PHOTOGRAPHY | FASHION | STAGE DESIGN | WINDOW DRESSING | ORNAMENT—all of it in lettering that was itself a manifesto for the modern style.

The real radicalism wasn't just the typeface. It was the combination of high art (painting, sculpture) with matters as commercial as shop window display; and, more particularly, the emphasis on the kinds of visual work that, in this new age, might be done by and for women. Which is perfectly in line with the most notable social innovation in the neighborhood: female education. The Reimann School was incidentally tilted toward women, but two other nearby institutions took this matter as their central charge. Both continue today, and both contribute to the neighborhood's architectural panorama. What began in the 1870s as an installation for the feeding of undernourished babies turned first into a day nursery on advanced principles of child-centered education and then, via the work of Alice Salomon, feminist and international activist, into the German Academy for Social and Pedagogical Women's Work. These projects were undertaken in the Pestalozzi Fröbel House (named for two of the childcare theorists), which still functions as a center where early education is both taught and practiced. The site itself is a must-see, not perhaps so much for what must be by now the very familiar Bavarian castle architecture as for the sequence of tiny exquisite sculptural scenes atop the building's fenceposts representing a variety of children's stories: take a walk down Karl Schrader Straße and see how many you can identify.

But the crowning glory of the birth of feminism in the Bavarian Quarter is the Lette Verein, founded in the 1860s for (in their words) the "Promoting of Higher Education and Gainful Employment of the Female Sex," where, by the 1920s, the subjects taught had transitioned from such highly traditional women's activities as domestic management and nursing to occupations that reflected the technological advancements of the modern world, like photography. It still operates as a training school in fashion and graphic design, but also in pharmacy and chemistry. And—more immediate to the point of our travels in the Bavarian Quarter—it operates in the set of buildings where it began in the early years of the twentieth century. So important was this set of activities from the earliest years of the neighborhood that Haberland's organization ceded prime space for it in Viktoria-Luise-Platz. Yet another Jewish architect with one foot in retro and another in the modern world, Alfred Messel, designed a gorgeous set of buildings for the Lette Verein, where it still stands. You may even now transport yourself from the relative quiet of Viktoria-Luise-Platz into the deeper quiet of the Verein's courtyards, each architectonically simpler and more bucolic than the one proceeding. But in your quest for simplicity, do not overlook the repeated, and often quite elaborately sculpted, emblems of the bee and the beehive: they represent the message of diligence that the Lette Verein was, and still is, teaching the pupils fortunate enough to belong within these gracious walls.

Moral of the story: the plutocracy that invented the Bavarian Quarter and the commercial bourgeoisie who made the kind of money that enabled them to live there understood that they had social responsibilities beyond the four walls of their own finely decorated flats. And it's this heady combination—Jews with money; a taste for opulently stylish design; a social consciousness oriented toward upward mobility via education—that still reads loud and clear as one rambles along these handsome thoroughfares.

Yet the truth of the matter is that neither the magnates nor the attorneys nor the social reformers nor perhaps even the architects would have brought our attention to the Bavarian Quarter were it not for the fact that during the first three decades of the twentieth century it housed an extraordinary collection of persons in the arts and sciences, in entertainment and literature—persons, in short, whom, if only there were time travel, we would most love to meet.

Not that they're all household names in the twenty-first century. I've become attached, for instance, to a now largely forgotten satirical writer who went by the name Alexander Roda Roda (Innsbrucker Straße 44). Partly it's because in his middle years he regularly performed in cabarets wearing a vest made from the bright red lining of the military uniform he wore before he was thrown out of the army for conduct "unbecoming an officer," whatever that may have been. But mostly it's because he composed the following "Brief History of Literature":

> One man alone: a lyric poem
> two men: a ballad
> one man and one woman: a novella
> one man and two women: a novel
> one woman and two men: a tragedy
> two men and two women: a comedy.

Try it out among your own favorite books.

Then there's Ilse Blumenthal-Weiss (Bamberger Straße 47), Schöneberg born and raised. I love the mutually supportive quality of her two professions: physical therapist and poet. Her life took her far from orthopedics and the Bavarian Quarter through the horrors and onward to Long Island. Living there quietly and writing verse inspired by all the death she witnessed, had she, I wonder, held on to the letter that Rainer Maria Rilke wrote her in 1921:

> I have an indescribable confidence in those peoples that have not come to God through belief but have experienced God through their own race, in their own stock. Like the Jews. . . . You have, *do not forget*, one of the greatest gods of the universe in your descent, a God . . . to whom one belongs, through one's people, because from time immemorial he made one and formed one in one's forefathers . . . ineradicably planted in Him, with the root of his tongue!

Vergessen Sie nicht!: easier for Rilke, ensconced in the *real*—rather than the *Jewish*—Switzerland when he wrote that letter, to insist that she guard her racial memory than it doubtless was for her, in the many future decades of her life.

It's perverse of me, perhaps, to enshrine a Bavarian Quarter painter, Kurt Dietrich Losch (Meraner Straße 12), who is so forgotten that his relatives recently put out an Internet notice begging for information about his life and works. But I memorialize him owing to a few lovely expressionistic watercolor cityscapes, to the fact that he kept painting while in the trenches of World War I, and the fact that as a middle-aged man, unable to make a living as an artist, he got reabsorbed into the giant family soap business.

A scant block from Losch, one could find two of the neighborhood's great educator-social reformers. Cora Berliner (Kufsteiner Straße 6) broke out of a customary girl's education to become a high-ranking economist in the Weimar Republic, while also contributing active support to women's movements within the educational organizations of the Jewish community. Luise Zickel founded a private girls' school (also in Kufsteiner Straße) along the same kind of progressive principles.

Their neighbor, Gottfried Benn (Bozener Straße 20), counts as Bavarian Quarter royalty. A physician as well as a poet, he had early *succès de scandale* with verses that exploited the most abject facets of his medical experience:

> The mouth of a girl who had long lain in the reeds
> looked so chewed up.
> When we broke open the torso, the esophagus was so
> full of holes.
> Finally in a bower under the diaphragm
> we found a nest of young rats.

Benn was the voice of a grimly disillusioned young generation following upon World War I. Then, a temporary, but apparently whole-hearted, embrace of the Nazi regime left him with his own lifelong abjection. First, he was vilified by fellow-authors who had gone into exile. Then the charm of the regime wore off for

him; he was denounced (inaccurately) as a Jew, "Benn" being per-
ilously close to the Hebrew "Ben," and he was effectively silenced.
This excommunication is no surprise, considering that he was
now writing poems like "Monologue," which begins

> Their guts fed with snot, their brains with lies,
> Chosen peoples now the jesters of a Clown,
> In games of chance, in stargazing and bird formations
> Trying to decipher their own filth.

It took several postwar decades, during which he quietly maintained his medical practice out of Bozener Straße, for something
like rehabilitation.

Long before those grim times, Benn had met another Bavarian
Quarter resident, Else Lasker-Schüler (Motzstraße 7), herself an
expressionist poet of mystic, orientalizing, and—increasingly,
as she grew older and sadder—Hebraic tastes. Her love poems
to Benn from the period of their liaison during the teens and
early twenties count as some of her least gloomy bits of pro-
duction ("Can you feel my essence | All around you | Like some
distant hem?"). The "Lasker" in her name came from her first
husband, whose brother counts as another of the neighborhood
stars. Emanuel Lasker (Aschaffenburger Straße 6a) was trained
as a mathematician and prided himself in his work as a philosopher. What he really was, however, was one of the greatest chess
players of all time, world champion for nearly three decades and
a certified international star. If you dip into the specialized literature of chess—in itself a hallucinating experience for someone
like me who can barely remember how to move a bishop—you
will discover that Lasker was, depending on whom you read, a
"psychological" or an "avant garde" or an "expressionistic" chess
player, any one of which suits the temperament of the neighborhood, whatever it may mean in chess.

There was, of course, more than local geography or family
connection that brought these inhabitants together. A short
walk would bring the avant garde denizens of the Bavarian Quarter to the Romanisches Café on the Kurfürstendamm, the habi-
tués of which—despite the notoriously bad food, which led to its

vernacular renaming as *Rachmonisches Café*, after the Yiddish for "pathetic"—read like a roster of twentieth-century greats: Bertolt Brecht, Max Liebermann, Alfred Döblin, Otto Dix, Stefan Zweig, just to pick a few who *didn't* live in the Bavarian Quarter. Else Lasker-Schüler hung out with one of her husbands (Herwarth Walden, who founded the enormously influential expressionistic journal *Die Brücke*) in the predecessor establishment, Café des Westens, also a brief stroll from our neighborhood, and then switched to the Romanisches Café and the company of Gottfried Benn. From a different stratum of the community, it was the meeting place of Ruth Klinger and Maxim Sakaschansky, who established the wildly successful Kabarett Kaftan (Martin-Luther Straße 31), where the entertainment was in comical Yiddish, and the sociological message was all about the class divisions separating the newly arrived, barely German-speaking Polish Jews from the assimilated bourgeois Berlin Jews who had nevertheless imbibed the romance of the millennial Hebrew heritage, not to mention the even greater gulf between either of those groups and the long established high-class Berliners of barely recollected Jewish origins who wouldn't be caught dead at the Kabarett. (Cf. my mother, summoning up her own yiddishkeit in reporting her encounter with a certain Mrs. Lehmann, of certifiable *alt-Deutsch* origins: "She's such a fency lady she puts on a het to take de gobbidge out.")

It's no coincidence, perhaps, that those Cafés were outside the boundaries of the Bavarian Quarter, whereas the other preeminent hub, smack in the middle of the neighborhood (Bayerischer Platz 13/14), was a bookstore. Except that there seems to have been a direct conduit—a not-so-underground railway, or perhaps the U4 itself—between the Romanisches Café and the Buchladen Bayerischer Platz, founded by Benedict Lachmann (Freisinger Straße 11) in 1919. It's a defining feature of Bavarian Quarter culture that this remarkable class of persons who ate, drank, and argued with each other at the Café went directly off to Lachmann's shop to buy books by the people they'd been arguing with. And there was plenty to argue about. Gottfried Benn was declaiming his nihilistic poetry in both places. Eduard Bernstein (Bozener Straße 18) was formulating the principles of the

Social Democratic movement. And Lachmann himself, while his shelves were stocked with a wide variety of aesthetic and political materials, was publishing his own tracts in a relatively far-out celebration of anarchism.

Books were everywhere in the neighborhood, of course. In 1929, the publishing house Rowohlt, which eventually made a fortune with its "ro-ro-ro" flimsy little paperbacks at incredibly low prices (the backbone of my affordable German library when I was in college), was forced to downsize and located itself at Passauer Straße 8/9, where a busy little coterie of literati were bringing into print authors—just to cite some familiar names—like Ernest Hemingway and Sinclair Lewis. One of the chief literary advisors in that workshop was Kurt Pinthus (Heilbronner Straße 2), whose own work stretched from expressionist poetry to cinema to theatrical collaborations with Max Reinhardt, and whose life spanned from the Bavarian Quarter to the Library of Congress.

If we take a little circuit from Benedict Lachmann's flat at the northeast corner of the neighborhood, we can soon encounter practitioners of other arts. Renate Schottelius (Rosenheimer Straße 12) began in the corps de ballet of the Städtische Oper to become, once exiled to the Americas, a central figure in the world exportation of modern dance, as stunning black-and-white photographs still attest. Another local who flourished as an adult outside Germany, and anything but in black and white, was the painter Lilli Gettinger (Barbarossa Platz 3), whose canvases are a multicolored mix of expressionism, memory, and exile. One final neighborhood child whose visual work, after the war, needs no introduction—now we're talking both black-and-white *and* color—is Helmut Neustaedter (Innsbrucker Straße 24), who practically invented our twentieth-century sense of visual decadence and the female form. We know him under the appropriately translated name Helmut Newton.

If it seems like cheating to cite these individuals who were driven out of the Bavarian Quarter, and Germany, while they were mere children, let us counter the objection proudly by declaring that the neighborhood knew how to nurture talents that were forced to develop elsewhere. But, among those with long residence there, let us also cite Carl Hofer (Grunewaldstraße 44), expressionist painter of the quotidian and the bizarre. His alienated souls, hauntingly lonely or lonely in pairs or dwarfed by props bigger than they are, look like they could benefit from the work of nearby neighbor Erich Fromm (Bayerischer Platz 1), whose socialist-humanist-pacifist psychoanalytic gospel seized the temper of the times decades later, with *The Art of Loving*. Back in the twenties, when he was operating out of his analytic studio in the Bavarian Quarter, he was still working out relations among the Talmud, the psyche, and the fabric of society.

And Fromm had plenty of colleagues in the streets around him. Judging, admittedly, from a small sampling, we might conclude that the Bavarian Quarter was the nursery of psychoanalytic radicals. Fromm veered off into humanism. Fritz Perls (Ansbacher Straße 13), with a background in experimental theater and regular visits to the inevitable Romanisches Café, swerved off into Gestalt. Wilhelm Reich (Schwäbische Straße 16) careened still farther into a psychoanalysis of sex and the body, culminating in the construction of his notorious orgone boxes—parodically immortalized in Woody Allen's *Sleeper* and dealt with far more grimly by the FDA, who sent him to Lewisburg Federal Penitentiary, where he died, having followed one of the more tortured routes of the twentieth-century diaspora.

Time for a change of pace. Athletes? Lilli Henoch (Treutlinger Straße 11, formerly Haberlandstraße 5) was a world record holder in track and field, while Alfred Flatow (Landshuter Straße 33) carried off gymnastics medals in the 1896 Olympics.

Or perhaps musicians. Kurt Weill needs no introduction, courtesy of *The Threepenny Opera*, "September Song," "Mack the Knife," etc., except to say that he spent a few months as the choir director in a Bavarian Quarter synagogue (Münchener Straße 37). He was the pupil of neighbor Ferruccio Busoni (Viktoria-Luise-Platz 11), whose compositional style spanned music history from Bach to the twelve-tone row; and later he was himself the teacher of the Chilean virtuoso Claudio Arrau (Stübbenstraße 8), whose big sound and big repertoire made an indelible impression on me during some of my first visits to Carnegie Hall. It's nice to think I was reaching out to the Bavarian Quarter, unknowingly, in 1955 and taking his recording of Beethoven's First Piano Concerto home with me to spin on my family's Victrola back in 14M.

Down the street from Arrau one might find Arno Holz (Stübbenstraße 5). Nowadays he gets called a great nature poet, but I knew him as the author of nasty little lyrics—he named them "Maxim verses"—that livened up my German class. His collection was called *Berliner Schnitzel* (get it—as opposed to *Wiener Schnitzel?*), and a once favorite poem of mine entitled "For Dessert" ran:

> Nicht jeder, der hinkt,
> Hat heut eine Chaise;
> Nicht alles was stinkt,
> Ist Limburger Käse.

Roughly:

> Not every gimp
> Gets a chauffeur;
> Not every stench
> Is a Roquefort.

I won't say it made as strong an impression as Arrau's Beethoven, but working out that set of equivalences—limping/limousines/Limburger—managed to stick with me.

A scant block away, Alfred Kerr (Bamberger Straße 32), ferocious drama critic nicknamed "The Culture Pope," practiced a prose style that was, indeed, something like Holz's poetic style, with one-line sentences, one-sentence paragraphs, and one-paragraph chapters. Reading him ("My work isn't literary criticism, it's ganglia criticism") is like reading a contractor's punch list. And he had plenty of punch: his feuds with Bertolt Brecht and Karl Kraus outlived exile and World War II. Apropos survival, let us not forget another of the neighborhood's giants: Billy Wilder (Viktoria-Luise-Platz 11). Granted, *Double Indemnity*, *Sunset Boulevard*, and *Some Like It Hot* appeared decades after he made his way out of the neighborhood. While he lived in the Bavarian Quarter, he doesn't seem to have gotten much further than a little journalism, a little experimental film-making, and (possibly) some action as a gigolo. Nobody's perfect.

Before any emigration to Hollywood, the iconic film of the Weimar period was surely *The Blue Angel*, scripted by Carl Zuckmayer (Fritz-Elsas Straße 18). A few clicks into YouTube and you can hear the star of *The Blue Angel*, Marlene Dietrich, who immortalized herself as the irresistible Lola Lola, gravely dangerous to the elderly professor, singing "Das war in Schöneberg":

> It was in Schöneberg,
> The month was May.
> There was a little maiden
> Who loved to kiss the boys.
> Which is customary
> In Schöneberg.

Circa 1913 this hit song doubtless brought hordes of lusty swains to the neighborhood. Not, perhaps, to the high-minded upper bourgeois Bavarian Quarter. Dietrich herself, though Schöneberg born and bred (and buried), grew up in a far more louche part of the district—the so-called Red Island, an urban triangle created by the construction of train lines. The composer of the song, Walter Kollo, was, however, Bavarian Quarter all the way (Schwäbische Straße 26), so perhaps he did know something about the *Mädelchen* who lived there. And he found a closer-to-home collaborator in the great chanteuse Claire Waldoff (Regensburger Straße 33), who actually gets mentioned in the Schöneberg song, their most famous joint venture being an operetta from which she took her Berliner dialect theme song: *Ach Jott, wat sind de Männer dumm* (Oh God, how stupid men are!).

Speaking of which, one near neighbor of Waldoff's was Egon Erwin Kisch (Hohenstaufenstraße 36), aka "The Raging Reporter," who made a name for himself throughout central Europe as an iconoclastic journalist. His real fame, however, came as a dedicated communist through and beyond the war years. And he deserves to be especially remembered for a seriocomic episode (worthy of Billy Wilder in his *Ninotchka* phase), when he was detained at sea outside Australia on grounds of his subversive activities, whereupon he gained entrance by jumping twenty feet from the ship to the dock, broke his leg, and was subsequently required by the Australian immigration authorities to take a language test in Gaelic (a spiteful gesture on their part). Unsurprisingly, he failed the test, but was ultimately successful in challenging the constitutionality of his exclusion, at which point he was able to address twenty thousand cheering Sydney antifascists.

Returning from the Southern Hemisphere to the Bavarian Quarter, consider what range of human imagination and experience crisscrossed there during a very few decades. Some were Jews, some weren't, some were mixed; some died before the Nazis, some at the hands of the Nazis, some survived; some remained, some were exiled, some returned. No need to tally the specific numbers: after all, I began by saying that the neighborhood was integrated, and now we can see that it embraced them all. My personal image—I haven't spent my life with Renaissance art for nothing—is the *School of Athens*, in which Raphael makes us believe that about a thousand years of antiquity and all the geniuses from Plato to Ptolemy to Averroës could be contained in one gorgeous (and, for him, modern) urban enclosure. The Bavarian Quarter comprises a far shorter time span, and the inhabitants are less famous. Still, to think that makers of operettas and of paperbacks, a passel of revolutionary shrinks and a pole vaulter, proponents of progressive education and borderline pornographic photography met, or narrowly missed meeting, each other in these very few square miles is to postulate the twentieth century's own School of Schöneberg.

But let us return to that word *genius*. Although I keep insisting that the Bavarian Quarter wasn't in any technical sense a ghetto, some stretches appear to have been more Jewish than others. Notably, the eponymous Haberlandstraße, which, as you may recall, had its name changed to avoid memorializing the founder's father. The *Jewish Address Book* turns up no fewer than sixty names grouped predominantly in half a dozen of the apartment houses on that brief stretch of thoroughfare. Looking down the list of Rosenthals and Nathansohns and Ginsburgs, one name rather stands out: *Einstein, Albert, Professor.*

With which we come to the neighborhood's most famous inhabitant. Einstein was not a native Berliner, like many of those we have met on these streets; he was born in the distant town of Ulm, in Southern Germany. But, whether early or late in his life, it would be difficult to pin him down geographically: his family moved to Munich when he was a baby, from which they had extended residences in Italy and Switzerland. For much of his life—and very fortunately—he held a Swiss passport.

None of which, admittedly, makes Einstein the quintessential Bavarian Quarter denizen, until we look at his life there a bit more closely. He lived for something like fourteen years at Haberlandstraße 5, making it quite possibly his longest continuous residency until he got to my own later-life hometown of Princeton, New Jersey. And it was a highly significant period for his achievements: the first proof (via a solar eclipse) of his theory of relativity; the beginnings of his work on quantum mechanics and the unified field theory; the Nobel Prize in Physics.

But these are not the things that bring him to our attention *here*. For all that Haberlandstraße turns out to have been heavily Jewish, neither religion nor ethnicity brought Einstein there. It was rather a set of circumstances that qualify him for the neighborhood in quite a different way. Only in recent years have we come to understand just how socially irregular his private life was. As his first marriage drifted into divorce—itself a bit scandalous—he was beset with serious illnesses and found himself nursed back to health by his cousin Elsa—who was, incidentally, his cousin twice over, on both his mother's and father's sides of the family, and with whom, as it happens, he had been carrying on an affair for years.

It was her parents (also Einsteins) who moved to the building in Haberlandstraße, and if Albert's residency there began as a rest cure, it transformed itself into a liaison with Elsa that had to be kept quiet, and thence into a proper marriage. Except—it gets better—that for several months it was an open question whether he would marry Elsa or her twenty-year-old daughter Ilse, who was, of course, also his double cousin. All these tempestuous stages of life were, in fact, signaled by moves to apartments on different floors of the building; and well into this period he maintained a fictional address at a pension outside the neighborhood for the sake of propriety. So Einstein, though he was no modernist poet or expressionist painter, was living a private life that smacked in its own way of Bavarian Quarter avant garde.

And yet, as with the residences of many other cutting edge figures on the local scene, the Einsteins' eventual apartment on the fourth floor, once their union was blessed and legal, came to reflect a high bourgeois domesticity such as would have made Georg Haberland proud. The building has been obliterated—though some occupants on an upper floor of the utterly banal block that replaced it have festooned their balcony with a banner reading $E = mc^2$ (Figure 2.5)—but, owing to the renown of the former inhabitant, we have some detailed, if not always consistent, recollections of the grand dwelling as it once was. Sixty years later, Konrad Wachsmann, architect of the Einsteins' summer house and eventual collaborator with Walter Gropius in America, offered quite specific recollections of a parlor, a dining room with radio, which was actually the classic Berliner Zimmer, as well as separate sleeping rooms for husband, wife, and the wife's daughter—not the once potential Mrs. Einstein, but her younger sister; Wachsmann pointedly says that he doesn't know whether Ilse slept in the apartment or not. Others remembered either one or two balconies, and Einstein himself sent a postcard of the building with arrows indicating so vast an extent of their space within it as to suggest exaggeration, or boasting.

There are many testimonies to the grandeur of these surroundings: carpets, draperies, the so-called Biedermeyer Salon with a grand piano (which managed as late as the summer of 1933 to make its way gradually to the Einsteins' place at the Institute for Advanced Study, at which it remains, leading me to ponder exactly how far his Bechstein stands from our similar-sized Bechstein at an opposite corner of Princeton—but let that pass). Within a few years these opulent arrangements were further expanded, as the attic level of the building was turned into habitable space, which became Einstein's personal refuge, including a study, a bedroom, and a library—all of which, since it had been converted without the necessary permits, Einstein himself had to justify by application to the relevant civic authorities. By way of contrast to the grand rooms below, this space was notably spartan—a chair, a table, bookshelves, some portraits of physicists, and, curiously, a spyglass with which he is said to have inspected both the heavens and the neighbors.

If all these contrasts between old and new, science and art, avant garde and bourgeois anchor the Einsteins in the Bavarian Quarter, what makes this identification even more persuasive is the public life that was lived in these apparently private spaces. If I am driven to indulge in Raphael-esque fantasies of a *School of Schöneberg* as suggested by all the inhabitants with varying degrees of fame whom I have previously enumerated, I really need go no further than the circle around Einstein.

The world came to his door. No surprise that his scientific colleagues—for instance, Otto Hahn, Walther Nernst, and the three Maxes (Born, Planck, and von Laue), all Nobel laureates—should be on his guest list. But individuals came from much farther afield, geographically and otherwise. Rabindranath Tagore came to talk to him about poetry and peace. When Charlie Chaplin visited Haberlandstraße, he was impressed by the deep emotional wellsprings of the genius who lived there, though, coming from the grandeur of the Hollywood Hills, he recalled the apartment as something worthy of the Bronx. Later, in the very un-Bronx-like surroundings of Pasadena, he hosted Einstein at the premiere of *City Lights*. Ruggiero Ricci, American violin prodigy, paid a call during his first European tour at age fourteen.

Music, indeed, was at the heart of many of these friendships, and not only those with professional musicians. Einstein was an accomplished violinist, and he played chamber music with fellow amateurs ranging from Werner Heisenberg to Queen Elizabeth of Belgium; he liked playing Haydn, Mozart, and the Chaconne from Bach's Second Partita in D minor. Among the greats of the concert stage, his circle of friends—Artur Schnabel, Edwin Fischer, Erich Kleiber—was of stellar caliber. Fritz Kreisler is supposed to have said to him, "You know, Albert, if you hadn't discovered this damn theory of relativity, you would have been my biggest competitor." And he loved to listen to music as well. Sitting in the front row at the debut of another prodigy, Yehudi Menuhin, he said to a friend, "Now I know that there is a God in heaven."

A similar list of luminaries in other fields were in the friend-ship circle: Max Liebermann, Gerhart Hauptmann, Benedetto Croce, Franz Kafka. But this all takes us, perhaps, a little too far from the neighborhood. The truth about Einstein and the Bavarian Quarter is that he really lived there among *its* luminar-ies. He was a customer at Benedict Lachmann's bookstore, from which he boarded the U-Bahn at Bayerischer Platz to get to the Prussian Academy in Unter den Linden. He discussed politics—probably within the shop—with the social democrat Eduard Bernstein. He took long walks with Emanuel Lasker; although he wasn't a believer in chess (it was too militaristic for him), he nevertheless composed a lovely tribute on the occasion of Lask-er's sixtieth birthday, calling him "a Renaissance Man, gifted with a limitless drive for liberty" and a stubborn attachment to the deductive, as opposed to the inductive, method. He regu-larly socialized with the dramatic critic Alfred Kerr, at concerts, at evenings hosted by the President of the Reichstag, Paul Löbe, and in the salon of his friend and physician, Janos Plesch. He was present for the premiere of a Carl Zuckmayer Wild West drama called *The Backwoodsmen* and for the performance of a rather more enduring piece, Kurt Weill and Bertolt Brecht's *Threepenny Opera*, though he declared that he went only because he was coaxed there by his stepdaughter Margot. He ordered his tea cakes from the Café Wittelsbach, conveniently located near both Lachmann's bookshop and the U-Bahn. He was world famous, but, in some important ways and for a decade and a half, the Bavarian Quarter *was* his world.

I love thinking of him as I make my way through the neigh-borhood. Quite apart from the fact that Einstein is the master-mind who revolutionized our conceptions of time and space, there is something about the man who was a pacifist in a bad war but a careful strategist during a good war, whose theories were responsible for a terrible weapon but who was tireless in warning the world about its dangers, who adhered to a humane version of socialism while maintaining an instinctual resistance to political extremism, who was a thoroughly secular Jew but warmly respectful of tradition, who campaigned actively for the establishment of the State of Israel but was profoundly prescient about the situation of the Palestinian people, who was the consummate pan-European but nevertheless became a loyal, and liberal, American, who loved Haydn and Mozart as much as he loved physics, who was domestic enough to use his theories to invent a new form of refrigerator while ordering his tea cakes from Café Wittelsbach. Granted, one cannot locate all these virtues in the Bavarian Quarter, neither then nor now, but as I walk these streets and contemplate the crazy mix of art and commerce, of bourgeois and radical, of Jew and gentile, during those long ago decades, I feel, if not exactly at home, then in a place I would like to call home. In all of this—and I'm afraid the pun is unavoidable—Albert Einstein remains the genius loci.

3

People: **Rahel Varnhagen**

The German national poet and magus, Johann Wolfgang von Goethe, visited Berlin exactly once, in May of 1778, and he didn't stay long. It was a city, he said, inhabited by a bold race of humans, where delicate manners were useless and where crudeness and rough speech were the only ticket to success. "The crowd," he wrote, "is blessed with cleverness and irony, and they're not stingy with these gifts." He compared the place to Sodom while also, somewhat inconsistently, declaring it to be a "prosaic city," where the demonic had little opportunity to manifest itself. As the creator of Faust's nemesis Mephistopheles, he knew from demonic, but—not very presciently—he didn't find it in Berlin. And he voted with his feet: for much of his life, he remained at the safe distance of Weimar, a couple hundred miles away.

To be sure, Goethe, born in 1749, is a man of the old school, and his opinions reflect the never-to-be-overlooked fact that Berlin is a radical latecomer on the European urban scene, not only in comparison to, say, London or Paris, but even as regards other German-speaking cities like Frankfurt or Vienna. No surprise, growing up when he did, that Goethe had a vision of the place as a cultural desert. He can be pardoned if he failed to notice that within his lifetime—a long span of eighty-two years—radical changes were taking place. By the end of the eighteenth century, Berlin was ablaze with aesthetic, philosophical, literary, and political excitement, becoming the favored place of residence, or at least of extended sojourn, for most of the boldface names that produced the grand confluence of neoclassicism and romanticism that made it a site for Germany's cultural golden age, competing only with the 1920s, when, once again, Berlin is at the center.

There can never be one single cause why certain times and places become the hub of change leading to what retrospect terms a golden age. Still, if it is permissible to pick out a single strand in this fabric, a gear in this machine, I would suggest we take a look at one individual, a Jew, who, while still in her twenties, unmarried and possessed of no extraordinary fortune or beauty, began exercising her influence over Berlin society in the last years of the eighteenth century by the sheer force of her sociability, or, as it was labeled in its own time, *Geselligkeit*: companionability.

Rahel Antonie Friederike Levin Robert Varnhagen—I offer up her lifetime litany of names, though henceforth she will be just "Rahel," with apologies lest that choice seem demeaning or overly familiar—is no stranger to the reading public. Beginning in the 1830s, her husband, who outlived her by twenty-five years, published multiple volumes of her correspondence, along with reminiscences by and about her friends. A hundred years later Hannah Arendt would produce a biography that is perhaps to be read less as a piece of scholarship than as a look backward from one significant moment in the history of Jews and Germans to another such moment. As regards our own time, Rahel is certainly in a position to benefit from the increased interest in women's writing, though she is only now beginning to receive the attention she deserves, even in the German-speaking world; and it continues to astonish me that there exists no English language edition that might offer a goodly sampling of her astonishing epistolary output.

That gap will not be filled here. Our focus will be on Rahel's place at the center of the salon life she superintended intermittently over a period of thirty-five years, and on the extraordinarily varied individuals who were her friends (Figure 3.1). Bottom line: if Berlin at the beginning of the nineteenth century was on its way to becoming a focal point of culture in realms from theater to statecraft, from theology to poetry, the phenomenon is to be observed at its greatest concentration by pursuing some of the city's loftiest representatives of the arts, the nobility, and the intelligentsia as they regularly sipped tea in a Jewess's house.

It was a cast of characters spanning the whole of Germanic culture, and beyond. Take, for example, Franz Grillparzer, some-

times considered Austria's national poet, also the author of bombastic political dramas and, in person, said to have been gloomy
and perhaps even misogynistic. Not so in the face of Rahel,
whom he met on a visit to Berlin in 1827. Dragged upstairs to her
apartment—she was frequently touted as a tourist attraction—
after a long day of socializing, Grillparzer sees an "aging woman,
who had probably never been pretty and was now bent double
with illness, like some fairy, not to say witch." But then she
"began to speak, and I was enchanted. My fatigue evaporated, or
rather gave way to a kind of drunkenness. She talked and talked
until practically midnight, and I still don't know whether they
led me away or whether I left of my own accord. I've never in my
life heard more interesting talk."

Grillparzer may have been introduced because of shared liberal views. Different politics and different profession in the case
of Leopold von Ranke, the father of modern history-writing. In
the 1820s he regularly made his way up those same stairs that
Grillparzer had been impelled to climb. About one such evening Rahel writes, "I remained at home reading. Happily. Not for
long. Ranke came, stayed until 10:00. Conversation about marriage. History." Like much of her writing, the notebook entry is
enigmatic. Would she have rather been alone? What does that
non sequitur "marriage. History" tell us about their conversation? And how did it happen that this brilliant young scholar
of a most scientific, not to say pedantic, inclination should be
discussing matrimony with a lady twenty-five years his senior?
A few months earlier, he interrupted his research on the *Lives of
the Popes* long enough to send her an Indian love poem, which,
she declares in her effusive letter of thanks, makes her think of
history. Rahel, it turns out, had a way of bringing poetry into
some rather prosaic places.

On to a personage who was anything but prosaic. During a
visit to Vienna, on the occasion of the 1815 Congress that was
dividing up Europe after Napoleon's defeat—everyone who was
anyone converged upon the city and its amusements during those
months, giving rise to the untranslatable witticism of another
of Rahel's friends that "le Congrès danse beaucoup mais il ne
marche pas"—Rahel paid a visit to none other than Beethoven.

In fact, they had encountered previously at Teplitz Spa, when the composer, despite his usual reticence, had accepted Rahel's invitation to play a private concert for her, causing a little whirlwind of gossip. Some have even said that Rahel was Beethoven's famously unidentified "Immortal Beloved." More likely, it was Bettina von Arnim, yet another intimate in the Rahel circle.

Something completely different: it may seem surprising that Ernst von Pfuel, a Prussian general who eventually rose to be War Minister and then Prime Minister of Prussia, should be a regular at Rahel's salon. Pfuel wasn't exactly regular army, though. We may wish to leave aside the fact that his friend Heinrich von Kleist (also, as we'll see, a Rahel habitué) was in love with him, exclaiming in letters, "I have often gazed at your beautiful body . . . with truly womanly feelings" and "you were designed on the model of the most beautiful young bullock that Zeus ever created." Still, it must be noted that Pfuel's lasting achievement was apparently less on the battlefield than in the swimming pool (where he is said to have invented the breast stroke). Rahel's salon was, of course, neither war zone nor natatorium, except perhaps metaphorically. But one witness there celebrated Pfuel for his ability to "uplift fiery zeal into the snow-capped realms of abstract contemplation." Which was a military gift in its own right, and doubtless indispensable at Rahel's tea table.

Consider another individual whose professional milieu was not nearly so remote from Rahel's: Mme de Staël. Relations between the parallel doyennes begin rather icily as early as 1800 in Paris. Rahel decides that what most interested de Staël about her was the fact that she had a Spanish lover: "She believes that the Spanish know how to love," Rahel muses in an 1804 letter, "God knows what idea she's got in her head about the daughters of Abraham!" When de Staël, now in Berlin, is told that Rahel would be a major attraction in *any* city, she explodes, "What pretension! A little Berlin girl who would create a stir in the circles of Paris!" A soirée is nevertheless arranged, including *le tout Berlin*. "As soon as they had been presented," the mutual friend reports, "Rahel sat Mme de Staël down in the corner of a sofa, where the two of them, all by themselves, talked for an hour and a half, without any concern for the entire rest of the company."

After this tête-à-tête, the conversion is complete, as de Staël declares, "I make abject amends for what I have said. You did not exaggerate at all. She is astonishing!"

One more member of the Rahel coterie whose origins lie even farther off than de Staël's. There appears in the salon one evening a young foreigner with an insatiable desire to learn everything from everyone. He has already copied the gist of Hegel's philosophy in a notebook. Loosed at one of Rahel's evening gatherings, he asks a painter to give him the principles of portraiture, a singer to explain how she projects her voice, a general (in fact, it's our amphibious friend Pfuel) to impart the rules for winning a battle. Who is he, and where does he come from? He is Albert Brisbane, from Batavia, New York. A fellow guest patronizingly records, "He was such an amazing, and in these parts, alien figure that a primordial human from those far-off regions, a veritable Redskin, would hardly have aroused more astonishment." Rahel, however, does not patronize him but rather takes him under her wing. The naïve young American, who will eventually, like a quite freakish number of his fellow upstate New Yorkers, found a utopian community, helps crystallize a progressive and egalitarian consciousness toward which Rahel's experience in the European upheavals from the French Revolution through Napoleon and on to the conservative restoration had been tending.

But Rahel *herself* cannot be seen only through the lens of her guests. She lived in proverbially momentous times (1771–1833), from the last days of the ancien régime through revolution, Napoleonic conquest, reactionary restoration, and onward into the days of the bourgeois monarchy. If that chronology is francocentric, it reflects the fact that Europe, and certainly Rahel's high-end milieu, was itself francocentric. One could also measure those sixty-odd years as mapping the cultural arc from the neoclassical to the romantic (even if within Rahel's circle they are uncannily intertwined) or, to touch upon another register, between a time when wealthy and/or educated Jews were a subatomic percentage of the population to a time when they were skyrocketing into a microscopic percentage.

Viewed from a different perspective, Rahel's life was exemplary of a certain social stratum well above the median, though well below the top: large, well-placed families (often, as in her case, with a despotic paterfamilias), entangled via marriage and friendship with other large, well-placed families; freedom to travel to cultural hotspots (the Paris of the Enlightenment, the Vienna of the 1815 Congress) or to spas (Karlsruhe, Teplitz), at all of which they were likely to meet others of a similar social stripe; freedom as well to engage in an aristocratic-style nonchalance as regards the marital and the extramarital. Rahel herself had several rather public love affairs and remained single until the age of forty-three, when she married a man much her junior. Karl Varnhagen von Ense, in fact, spent the rest of his life making something of a career out of being Rahel's husband (eventually, widower), an act of self-subordination that did not go uncriticized. In the run-up to her marriage, she converted to Protestantism, a move she had contemplated in regard to previous potential husbands; this, too, was not unusual, and it needs to be viewed in broader social terms, though it may be difficult to say where each individual case fits as between mere expediency and profound conviction.

What cannot be captured in these contextual mappings is her sheer ubiquity: she knew everyone, everyone knew her, she visited everyone, everyone visited her. To call her an early nineteenth-century Zelig is to beg the insidious question whether Zelig is somehow an intrinsically Jewish fantasy.

We'll get back to Rahel's ubiquity soon enough. But there is another uniqueness that claims our attention as well. At a moment when writers of fiction are beginning to explore the riches of individual character, when Goethe, to pick a highly relevant example, is electrifying a European readership with complex personalities like Werther and Wilhelm Meister, Rahel appears to many of those around her like a piece of living literature. And, one after another, they seek to capture her in writing. These are remarkable documents, some of them reminiscing about a whole lifetime of connection with Rahel, others chronicling a single evening in her company. They are frequently endowed with a novelistic eloquence, doubtless inspired by the eloquence of their central figure, such that at times one feels oneself on a byway in the midst of literary history from Balzac to Proust during some little-known encounter they had at a café on Unter den Linden.

In this Berlin-based novel, collectively composed during the first three decades of the nineteenth century, the heroine is petite, a bit shapeless, and universally agreed to be "pleasant looking" rather than beautiful (see Figure 3.1). Several of the portraits place her eyes rather far apart: that feature, plus what appears to be a prominent nose (real, or an icon of an ethnic identification?), give her a look that is penetrating and reflective at the same time. The scenery around her consists of a series of not very grand domestic spaces. Beginning in the 1790s, it's an attic room within the Levin family lodgings, where a spartan tea is served on a weekly basis. As the story gets told, this becomes a kind of golden age, which comes to an end when Prussia is defeated by Napoleon in 1806 and Berlin becomes something of an occupied city. Although there are mournful accounts, from Rahel herself and the circle around her, of this change, and there are alterations in her marital status and geography over the succeeding years, the salon—peripatetic over the distance of a few blocks in Berlin Mitte, as we'll later observe—continues to flourish, albeit changing with the times, almost up to the time of her death. Indeed, there are some signs that its later incarnations become grander and more institutionalized, involving, for instance, actual food and wine.

It's not the place, however, but the person that captivates Berlin. And she is best captured in the words of the authors themselves. They tend to explode in sequences of acclaim, as though it's impossible to find the right word, or enough words, to praise her: "spirit, feeling, thought, image, wit, or insight—inspiring, shocking, instructive, ecstatic"; "independence of spirit, intensity of feeling"; "wit, profundity, discretion, genius, or just oddity and fancifulness"; "profundity and frankness, imagination and irony"; "she always knew how to liven up dullness, to interrupt offensiveness, to correct disturbance, to impart pleasure"; "I was lifted to the sphere of poetry, and that was done by what one might commonly call anti-poetical means, by reality in place of illusion, things in place of appearances—in a word, by truth."

In all this volume of literary reportage there is a fundamental paradox. Rahel may have been born to the People of the Book, but she published no books; and if she composed something approaching ten thousand letters, it only proved that her supreme verbal medium was somehow private, intimately connected with her talent for friendship—a social network, as it were, avant la lettre.

The actual tokens of this network—that is, her enormous epistolary output—are almost impossible to describe. Passionate introspection; long dream narratives; pontifications running the gamut from High Enlightenment to romanticism, often about the special status that she and the letter's addressee share, whether it's gender, religion, or world view; non sequiturs; words underscored one, two, or three times; anatomies of her relationship with the recipient, whoever he or she might be; and repeated complaints that she hasn't received enough communications in reply.

The letters may afford us a glimpse of her famous barrage of conversation, yet the writing and the speaking were clearly not the same. It is instructive to observe one of her admirers wrestling with the problem of capturing Rahel's presence, citing the most famous nonpublisher of all time: "I promised once in jest to collect her conversations, the way Plato did for Socrates." He declines to do so, but in the process he recognizes that the historical parallel isn't just about one individual speaking and another individual writing it down. Rather it's all about the profound influence that one person's speech can have on another person's life:

> These precious words of the greatest spiritual wisdom don't just live in my memory; rather they have passed over into the core of my deepest feelings, they have become my own unique ways of thinking. . . . She read into my soul, as though it were an open book with wide margins into which she added her own annotations and improved it on every page.

That metaphor of the book haunts these accounts of Rahel (who is herself quoted as saying "I'm no writer"), but never more powerfully than here, where she both reads and writes the book of her dear friend's life. We should recall that, while strolling by the river with Phaedrus, Socrates vowed to write on his friend's soul. Rahel was accomplishing the Socratic goal in multiples.

These talents were exercised over a vast field of persons, among whom the overarching figure, though he never set foot in any of her salons, was (to return to where we began) Goethe. Given the profoundly sociable nature of Rahel's spirit, it is another defining irony that she should have had so little face time with its presiding genius. A few direct sightings did, over the years, take place. There was an early encounter in Karlsbad, when Goethe pronounced her "a beautiful soul," then later some more ceremonial visits, in her husband's company, in Frankfurt and Weimar. In a characteristic act of self-promotion, Varnhagen was also bold enough to send Goethe a set of comments on the Master's work that had appeared in letters the married couple had sent to each other. No names were included, but they were credited to two different parties, "G" (Rahel) and "E" (Varnhagen). Goethe's quite enthusiastic response makes it clear where his preference lies. "E," he says, is of the tribe of those who "distinguish, examine, separate, and judge," whereas "G"—and this comes to be very often quoted about Rahel—"is of a remarkable, perceptive, uniting nature. . . . She does not really judge the object, but rather possesses it, and insofar as she doesn't possess it, it simply does not concern her." All of which might be said about the people, as well as the books, in her life.

And that parallel may be the decisive one. Rahel was, of course, an assiduous reader of Goethe; and a particular subset of his works, especially those where powerful emotions get framed within neoclassical restraints, gets cited continually in her correspondence and her conversation. But what may be more important for an understanding of Rahel as a cultural figure is that she embodied, by whatever definition she and her contemporaries understood the matter, a Goethean worldview in social practice: all-embracing in its range of interests, learned and yet lyrical, passionate and yet steeped in the Enlightenment.

It should be recalled that Goethe, especially in his younger years, was not immediately taken to be the supreme genius that he would eventually exemplify for the German-speaking world;

there was a little too much *Sturm und Drang* in the early work, with the pan-European viral career of *Werther*, including an epidemic of love suicides, doing him little good in the eyes of some eighteenth-century tastemakers. But by the time that Rahel was an established figure in Berlin, those who visited her understood that Goethe was a divinity and that her salon was his temple. Already in 1801 we hear one admirer declare, "About Goethe she spoke words of admiration that outclassed anything I've ever heard." And later, when Varnhagen celebrates her as the culmination of all virtues, the description is sourced quite specifically. These remarkable talents, he says, emerge as "little unexpected and gracious gestures, which together make up life itself and which, according to the judgment of Goethe, touch the deepest heart of things." In the monumental world of Goethe's fame, then and now, it is generally not little gestures, but very grand ones, that define his reputation; what Rahel's husband is actually saying is that she has transformed the Great Man's lofty wisdom into an everyday social practice.

We're speaking here of a significant entity referred to as the "Goethe cult." Whatever the concept may be taken to mean, and however the matter may have been debated then and now, Rahel has often been understood as its originator, or at least its epicenter. No surprise that one of her closest admirers should say, "Between her and Goethe existed an elective affinity of spirit and disposition." The expression loses something in translation: *Elective Affinities*, or *Wahlverwandschaften*, is the title of a particularly complex novel of Goethe's (in my view, one of his greatest works, though not an easy read), in which mysterious, quasi-chemical forces of attraction operate in a state of tension with such real world forms of union as bourgeois marriage. Rahel, as it happens, didn't care for *Die Wahlverwandschaften*—perhaps it hit a little too close to home—but the underlying tribute consists not only in treating Rahel as though she were herself a book by Goethe, but also in the suggestion that she and Goethe themselves constitute an elective affinity; if that is the case, they are disseminating their union via the salon and the extended friendship circle.

Extended indeed. One scholarly census of Berlin salons in

the long nineteenth century counts ninety-nine documentable guests chez Rahel, and I can think of a few to add to that number. Her various gathering places, in other words, saw a good deal of traffic. More striking than the sheer numbers, though, is the range of worlds that converged upon her. The theater, to begin with, was a prime source of persons and conversation topics. She was a close friend of Friederike Unzelmann, who starred in works by the likes of Shakespeare, Mozart, and Schiller. She worshipped the great actor Johann Friedrich Fleck, who also possessed a Shakespeare and Schiller repertoire, and was the object of a cult himself. She seems to have been the best frenemy of the enormously powerful producer August Wilhelm Iffland— attacking him in private, but inviting him to her soirées—whose fame persists today in the eponymous Iffland Medal, awarded to the greatest living German actor, currently Bruno Ganz (good choice!). She gossiped with a number of younger actresses, including Auguste Brede and Karoline Bauer, and she socialized with singers, among them Anna Milder and Henriette Sontag.

These may be forgotten names, especially outside the German-speaking world; not so Rahel's circle within the field of philosophy. Friedrich Schleiermacher was a close friend, as were both Humboldt brothers—Wilhelm the language philosopher and Alexander the naturalist. Johann Fichte the idealist was known to her via his son Immanuel, and Herder was treated to a panegyric about her by another mutual friend, who declares, "She is able to teach so gloriously and vividly because she herself hasn't learned anything, rather she has received it all with a chaste soul from the god within us, as a revelation of reason." These virtues may or may not have impressed Herder, but they certainly embody an eighteenth-century ideal.

The public sphere was also well represented, beginning with royalty in the person of one of her most frequent guests, Prince Louis Ferdinand, nephew of Frederick the Great, military figure, composer of chamber music, and the dedicatee of Beethoven's Third Piano Concerto. Nor was Louis Ferdinand the only military man. We've heard about General von Pfuel (the "beautiful young bullock" of Kleist's love letter). Also in attendance were Peter von Gualtieri, the Kaiser's Wing-Adjutant, Guards officer

Otto von Schack, and Luis Fernández de Córdova, staunch royalist general and, for a while, ambassador to Berlin. At a more reflective end of the public spectrum, the whole range of post–French Revolution political thought found aid and comfort in Rahel's circle.

In a sense—and the "cult of Goethe" has something to do with it—all those who sojourned under Rahel's roof became in effect literati. And literature itself was represented by a whole succession of major early nineteenth-century figures. With Friedrich von Schlegel and Ludwig Tieck as her close friends, for instance, Rahel could be seen as the godmother of German Shakespeare, canonized—indeed, naturalized as Teutonic—by the collaboration of that pair of writers as translators. Later in her life, she was close to an entire generation of romantic writers, including Friedrich de la Motte Fouqué, Clemens von Brentano, Adalbert von Chamisso, and the giants Heinrich von Kleist and Heinrich Heine. Indeed, with her strong formation in Goethe and classicism, her discourse became for many younger writers the conversation that bridged the Enlightenment and romanticism.

This roll call of names doesn't quite capture Rahel's world: like everyone else, she exists in a nexus of multiple interconnections, only more so. Friedrich Schlegel is brother to August Wilhelm Schlegel; August Wilhelm is married to Dorothea, whose first husband was the brother of Rahel's childhood friend David Veit, and she is herself the daughter of Moses Mendelssohn, whence the whole Mendelssohn clan, including the composer and his sister, become part of the story. Bettina von Arnim, besides her possible identity as Beethoven's "immortal beloved," is the sister of one member of Rahel's circle (Clemens von Brentano), married to another (Achim von Arnim), and conducting a long-term affair with yet another (Count Hermann von Pückler-Muskau). Not to mention her early liaison with Goethe. And speaking of liaisons, Rahel herself has significant affairs with at least two men (a Prussian Count, a Spanish diplomat) before marrying Varnhagen.

Not that all the entanglement is erotic. In this milieu, there is no end of professional crossover: actors consort with playwrights, political theorists debate other political theorists, poets love or hate other poets. But it ought to be no surprise that the salon is a world of women-in-charge, insofar as that is possible in 1800, and that one of the consequences is the special way in which the circumstances of private life, including marriage, family, and love affairs, play a formative role in the experience of some very public (and usually male) figures.

When Rahel's contemporaries set about to describe how she operated in this friendship circle—and they did so very often—the word *Paradoxie* comes up again and again. In part, they may have been thinking about an unexpected or playfully contradictory turn of phrase, such as we've already seen when she joins marriage with history as though they were the same thing or when she mixes "wit, profundity, discretion, genius" with "oddity and fancifulness." This sort of conversation must have produced a kind of double take in her listeners.

Such *Paradoxie* does not come without its share of tension and drama among the participants. The regulars, after all, included some quite difficult people. Rahel's brother, Ludwig Robert, who had a whiff of exotic scandal behind him—he fell in love with a famous (married) beauty and used his family's fortune to buy her divorce from her doltish first husband—exercised a depressing consciousness on her salon evenings and insisted on reciting his own lengthy poems, a practice that even his sister admitted to finding embarrassing. Rahel was partial to a certain Major von Schack; at one sad moment she bitterly comments that he is among the few who remain in her circle, while a couple of years later, at another sad moment, she lists him mournfully as among the dead ("fort, weg, todt"). But, as whispered salon conversation did not hesitate to point out, he was notorious for his habit of seducing very young girls (from the nobility, yet!) and for his cutthroat play at the card table, reducing one opponent to penury and suicide, news of which he received with complete indifference. Irony or just deserts: he, too, would die by his own hand.

The prolific writer Friedrich von Gentz, who at first was excited by the French Revolution and then, having read Edmund Burke, turned bitterly against it (would you believe that one of his books was translated by America's own John Quincy Adams?), was something of a powder keg in Rahel's coterie, occasioning groans from certain quarters the moment he came in the room. The reaction was not only for his political views but also because he was given to grand romantic outbursts ("I can't bear it any longer! What exhaustion, what agony! Writing, worrying the whole night through! Since 5 A.M. besieged by creditors, wherever I go they confront me, they badger me to death, never a moment's peace!") Similarly intense, if somewhat oddly directed passions regarding Rahel herself, as he expressed in an often quoted letter to her: "You are an *infinitely productive* creature, I am an *infinitely receptive* one; you are a great *man*, I am the first among *women*."

Prince Louis Ferdinand was another kind of problem child. It was doubtless a mark of distinction that the nephew of Frederick the Great should be so frequent a visitor to Rahel's salon (one visitor, presumably with amazement, notes that the Prince seats himself directly next to his Jewish hostess on the sofa), but behind his royal back other regulars gossiped endlessly about the way he was throwing his life away instead of using his talents for the general good. (No one seems to have been satisfied that he spent his time composing charming piano trios.) And the many-years-long and quite public affair he conducted with one of Rahel's best friends didn't do him, or his hostess, much good.

Indeed, the fact that the Rahel circle was something of a free love zone doubtless contributed to its social precariousness. Irregular romantic arrangements (including Rahel's own history and her special friendships with men like Gentz) were the rule rather than the exception. Scandalous books like Friedrich Schlegel's *Lucinde* were openly discussed; and, since it was thought to mirror the author's own love affair with Dorothea Veit prior to their marriage, these scandals were essentially being lived, as well as written about, in the Rahel milieu. Off-color jokes were occasionally told among the men, with Rahel herself (to everyone's surprise) joining in. Indeed, the atmosphere in the salon itself was full of edgy flirtation, involving attractive women like the actress Unzelmann or Rahel's beautiful sister-in-law, who not only had a gossip-worthy romantic history but was also the object of amorous verse by another of Rahel's friends, Heinrich Heine. And above all, her close friend Bettina von Arnim was a continual source of romantic innuendo, for instance when she revealed the name of her current lover to the whole assemblage by having herself announced not by her own name but by his, when he was in fact a hundred miles away. Love affairs, in short, were the subject of risky acting out.

Liaisons dangereuses were a problem when viewed from the more restrictive social rules outside this circle, but it was the fighting on the inside that represented the biggest challenge to Rahel's peaceable kingdom. Córdova, Spanish ambassador and general, was a flashpoint for arguments with the predominantly progressivist members of the company, especially when the subject of constitutional monarchy was raised by the likes of the liberal jurist Eduard Gans. The elderly Freiherr von Reden, described by one observer as talkative but so eloquent and well meaning "with an overflowing heart" that no one could take offense, nevertheless set Rahel's argumentative brother into a verbal brawl. The roller coaster ride of French politics, from the Revolution to Napoleon and beyond, was always good for a fight, with Rahel herself approvingly pronouncing the French people to have the republican idea in their very bones.

Besides arguments about politics there were arguments about having too many arguments about politics. Gans himself was one of the offenders, along with one Friedrich von Meyern, author of a forgotten five-volume orientalist novel called *Dya-na-sore*, who could talk of nothing but Napoleon and war, and who had to be diplomatically silenced. When they weren't arguing politics, they were arguing art, sometimes at the high levels of Schiller's aesthetics and other times at the level of scrappiness between partisans of different actresses or composers.

Nor did they all like each other. Regulars regularly complained about other regulars. The Protestant clergyman and philosopher Friedrich Schleiermacher, though he was an apostle of sociability—having, according to some, composed his *Essay on a Theory of Social Behavior* under the inspiration of Rahel's public ethos—criticized her for the indiscriminateness in her choice of companions, to which she replied that you wouldn't know what a good book was unless you read some bad books. Clemens von Brentano and Wilhelm von Humboldt, both of them intermittent members of the inner circle, thought that the choice of guests was too promiscuous and the conversation sometimes too free. And then, from the other end of the social scale, there is the preciously dystopic testimony of the actress Karoline Bauer (we'll hear more about this delicious memoir), who delights in presenting the clay feet of many of the Rahel circle idols. Varnhagen himself was a servile flatterer and gossip—Bauer paints a memorable picture of him "schnitzeling" the newspaper with scissors to collect bits of scandal for his notebooks—who had never uttered three little words: "I was wrong." August von Schlegel was effeminate and vain; Adelbert von Chamisso was silent, unkempt, and hypochondriacal; Brentano would never stop talking about his migraines and about the peace to be found in a Catholic cloister; Alexander von Humboldt was a "Paris-ified Salon man" who wore tattered clothes, his talk bubbling up like a fountain of cologne. And—unkindest cut of all—Bauer finds the whole Goethe Cult (which she names as such) a ridiculous piece of idolatry.

Rahel herself could be among the sharpest tongued of these complainers. "My reproaches," she says to one of her closest confidantes, "I reserve for my dearest friends." But in fact she spread these quite widely. She is the most outspoken critic of Prince Louis Ferdinand, declaring privately that he was living in a state of distraction and dissipation, lacking any firm and purposeful occupation. And when her brother complains about a tiresome old blowhard, more or less in the gentleman's very presence (after all, the room wasn't so very huge), Rahel rolls her eyes and declares,

> Don't you think I want to despair when I see him coming in? Don't I weep when he hangs around interminably? Have you forgotten how I quake at the mention of his name? But what can I do? I can't just show him the door, and I cannot tolerate anyone abusing or mocking him in my house, and the same goes for the [unidentified] Baron, whom my entire acquaintance loathes and who is abhorrent to me and yet who keeps coming here endlessly.

This combination of tolerance and intolerance is one of the hallmarks of Rahel's hospitality.

Rahel managed this motley crew via a complex game of insight, acceptance, and critique. Countless witnesses attest to her deep and almost instantaneous perception about their nature. Upon first meeting, one friend remembers that "during our lively conversation she kept playing with an eyeglass, and quick as lightning she would put it up to her eye and fix upon me." That image of swiftness runs through many of the accounts: "Lightning-speed insight into human beings," says a close friend, and another declares, "She gave me a look that pressed to my innermost being, and from which no bad conscience could be concealed." Yet another member of the circle, looking back on many years of her acquaintance, reflects on a consequence of all this exposure: "Everything that one said to Rahel was a confession, whether voluntary or not."

In fact, it's never very far from a kind of mass love affair, ever on the edge between Platonic and passionate. "I was tied to her irrevocably," says her French admirer the Marquis de Custine, "without being in love." To her Swedish friend Brinckmann, she declares that she wants to be both his *Freundin* and his *Freund*. And, around the time of her marriage to Varnhagen, she reassures Brinckmann, "It doesn't mean anything as far as you're concerned. I've never been freer than I am now."

Passions, or their simulacra, are capable of bursting out of the private realm and into the salon. At a moment of ideological warfare—the liberal Schlegel has attacked the conservative Gentz as a "corrupt scribbler and enemy of freedom"—Rahel shifts the entire register away from politics and toward Schlegel's secret love affair, which she both exposes and embraces. When the cliché of blind love is mentioned, she explodes the whole idea: "On that topic, I alter the whole mythology. Amor is *not* blind and carries no blindfold. On the contrary, he cures all blindness. Love sees clearly and sharply. The fact that Love proceeds onward in spite of everything it sees, that is its ultimate hallmark." A remark that doubtless reminded many of the listeners that Rahel was the embodiment of *Paradoxie*; a smaller number may have realized it was uttered for the sake of Gentz, with whom she was herself at this point in some kind of blind love.

It wasn't always love that she deployed to smooth over political eruptions. Quite frequently, there would be recourse to music. In an atmosphere rife with appreciation of Haydn, Mozart, and Beethoven, or debates about the relative merits of Rossini and Spontini (Rossini and *who?*), it's perhaps no surprise that our hostess would quite strategically summon up musical performance or discussion when the going got rough. At one salon visit in 1830, General Córdova—as we have seen, an absolutist of the old school—forsakes all his objectionable politics and turns himself into a musical aesthete just to please Rahel; now, the narrator of this evening tells us, all his warfare was on behalf of Rossini.

Sometimes Rahel's peace-making was achieved with laughter: "She cleared the stuffy air with sudden flashes of a gentle humor, so completely in her own style that I can only describe the surprise of them as a pleasant terror, a tiny shockwave with a mixture of wonderment and pleasure." The same observer goes on to compare her to the figure of the Fool in tragedy, who "softens the severity of impact through humor and in the process makes the cleverest comments." Most of all, though, it was her language itself, whether humorous or terrifying, that reigned supreme: "Who loved, indeed idolized Wit as she did?" "Her conversation was volatile, sharp, oblique." "Like brilliant fireworks . . . dazzling, impressive, seductive . . . numbing, unsettling."

In the end, though, one comes back to paradox. And perhaps the overriding paradox is that she was the mistress of a grand salon, but that what was most magnetic about her was the sense of her passionate connections with individuals. All of which gets summed up in the remarks—themselves quite witty—of two of her dearest friends. They deserve to be rendered in their original languages:

> *Sie kam, sie sprach, sie siegte.*
> *Du génie au service de l'intimité.*

She came, she spoke, she conquered: that is the Jewess from practically nowhere who mastered the world with the brilliance of her speech. *Genius in the service of intimacy*: that is the individual who made each of her many close companions feel as though they were uniquely blessed by her friendship.

It wasn't, to be sure, all utopic all the time. In 1810, when Rahel meets Heinrich von Kleist—arguably, the greatest literary genius among her close acquaintance—she doesn't know what to make of him. It's a moment of incipient romance for her, not with Kleist but with their mutual friend Alexander von der Marwitz, to whom she writes, "I'm quite struck by [Kleist]," but she adds, "Not a ray of tenderness in his eye, nor any sense of security." Meanwhile, to Varnhagen (with whom her romance is currently progressing toward eventual marriage), she writes of Kleist, "I love him, and what he's doing. He is true, and sees true." Within a year or so Kleist has put a gun in his mouth and pulled the trigger, in a suicide pact with Henriette Vogel. No romance between the two of them—Kleist, though he kept contemplating marriage (not with Henriette), had, as we have seen, unorthodox erotic sympathies—but rather a mortal folie à deux that ended on the shores of the Wannsee.

Marwitz is himself, as it happens, of a somewhat suicidal bent, though he actually meets his end in battle three years later. And when Rahel writes him about Kleist's death, in the earliest notice we have of this event, two days after it took place, the document is a masterpiece of coding and confusion (suicide, after all, was both a civil and a theological crime); she asserts at once that she and Marwitz have never discussed the topic with each other and yet she knows they think alike about suicide, for which she cautiously proceeds to offer some justifications, in terms reminiscent of *Hamlet*. Ironically, it's Kleist, in the one letter we possess from him to Rahel, who is attempting to cheer *her* up. This whole epicycle in the orbit of Rahel serves to remind us that the self-destructive side of romanticism—the heritage, as we might call it, of Werther—remains alive among our heroine's glittering array of friendships and closely tied to the persistently ambient eros.

Catastrophes aside, there were always problematic undercurrents in Rahel's celebrated companionability. Count von Salm, one of our most eloquent informants regarding life in the salon, records a conversation with her after the first evening he enjoys in her company. Ecstatic with pleasure at the hours he has spent among her acquaintanceship, he blurts out something about how happy she must feel at the center of this society. Her reply tells a different story:

I get no personal satisfaction from any of them. They bring me
their pains, their hurt feelings, their worries and woes. Their need
for conversation leads them here; and if they should find a better
outlet somewhere else, they'd leave me right away. I amuse them,
help them, listen to them, set them straight. . . . The profit is all
on their side. . . . I despise the conventions of good manners, the
formalities of friendships that have to be performed along official lines, to all of which I accord no value when they don't arise
altogether freely from the pure initiative of a good heart. . . . Shall
I confess one more thing? Among all the people you saw at my
home last night, there is only one whom I truly *like*, and this one
you probably won't have noticed.

There's no knowing who that special friend was: after all, if it's
true that Salm didn't notice him, he won't have figured in the
account of the evening that precedes this outburst. A consider-
ation which reminds us (as in every reconstruction of the past)
that our knowledge is limited by a telephone game of retell-
ings. Did Salm really possess total recall of a two-hundred-word
speech? Or, given the shapeliness of his narrative, was this rather
the appropriate novelistic turn in a short story that hardly represents the "real" Rahel at all? No knowing. In the end what most
authenticates this expression of melancholy is the wistful turn
at the end. Whoever the "only one" might have been (and the
gender is specifically masculine), the voice of Rahel rings true in
the *Paradoxie* of the opposition between the glittering company,
to whom she gives a great deal more than she receives, and the
far less voluble individual with whom, perhaps, she wishes she
were alone.

A quite different witness comes to a similar conclusion after
watching Rahel perform in her salon:

Hour after hour at her writing desk, or in front of her visitors, or
at the tea table, to be brilliant and original—at whatever cost!
Just like the job of the Delphic oracle, sitting at her tripod over
the steamy crevice of the earth, chewing laurel leaves, babbling
out divine mystical sayings to the waiting faithful, whether the

god or the spirit moved her or not. So many times my soul grieved for the adored Rahel when she sat there, pale, tired, racked with gout and angina, tortured in front of her tripod of a tea table, with numbing incense mounting on all sides, while her high priest Varnhagen was at his most eager and cruel, constantly giving her new chewable laurel leaves to slice between her teeth, and all eyes and ears fixed on her oracular mouth.

The ever candid Karoline Bauer doubtless captures something of the truth about Rahel that eluded the elegant gentlemen who were, in a different way, in her thrall. No surprise, perhaps, that it took an actress to recognize how, at the center of it all, was a woman engaged in playing a role.

Can we relive Rahel in the twenty-first century the way we summoned up past lives from the Schönhauser Allee cemetery or the Bavarian Quarter? I can assure you that Berlin remains a place of ardent conversation, where party politics, the latest *Regietheater* setting of Mozart in needle park, nostalgia for the divided city wittily termed *Ostalgie*, newly discovered unorthodoxies of hair, piercings, tattooings, or gender assignment, and the best place to get Currywurst (correct answer: no place—a mealy sausage dowsed in ketchup is not a pleasant experience) animate every contemporary gathering. But in case you're not on those guest lists or you prefer Rahel's world to our own, there is an exercise that can help in locating her in the streets of the city today. Take a map of Mitte—the heart of the East, including Unter den Linden, Museum Island, and the Brandenburg Gate—but forget about all those landmarks—and place a dot on each of the locations where Rahel held court during her long career, as follows:

Jägerstraße 54 (Figure 3.2)
Charlottenstraße, corner of Krausenstraße
Behrenstraße 48
Behrenstraße 45
Französische Straße, corner of Friedrichstraße (Figure 3.3)
Mauerstraße 36

You will have described a slightly ovoid shape, and that is going to be your territory for summoning up Rahel's world out of oblivion.

Inside that circle—think of it as something like Rahel's circle of friends—you will find the locations of both Rahel's salons. You will find four different residences of Heine, including Taubenstraße 32, where he spent his last sickly days, opposite the building where, three-quarters of a century earlier, Voltaire had stayed, and in which Friedrich Schlegel later resided. You will find a brace of von Humboldts: Alexander was born at Jägerstraße 22, and his brother Wilhelm held intellectual sway at Behrenstraße 30. You will find Schleiermacher (he of the finicky reaction to Rahel's other guests) in a multitude of places, including his well-preserved house at the corner of Taubenstraße and Glinkastraße (Figure 3.4). You could meet the whole Felix Mendelssohn-Bartholdy family at Leipzigerstraße 3, or encounter Achim von Arnim and Clemens Brentano as roommates (von Arnim enjoyed May mornings in the garden) at Mauerstraße 34. Iffland the impresario had his office in Französische Straße 44, Gaspare Spontini, Rossini's big competition, resided at Markgrafenstraße 48, with Rahel's predecessor and rival, Henriette Herz, holding forth at nearby No. 59 (Figure 3.5), and Kleist could have been found in a couple of different furnished rooms, including Mauerstraße 53, from which he traveled to his self-inflicted death scene, more of which anon.

I list all of these as though they were available for your viewing pleasure; in fact, apart from Schleiermacher's house, not a single building inhabited by these luminaries is still standing. The walk isn't entirely fruitless, though. The farthest stretches of this circle scarcely amount to more than half a mile, and since you will be using the only means of transport whose rate of progress hasn't changed since 1800—your legs—you will discover that Rahel's circle covered about ten minutes walk in Berlin. No wonder that via Rahel they were so tangled in each others' lives.

If you hunger for something more real, one option is to take the S-Bahn out to Wannsee, not the same conveyance that Kleist must have used in 1811, but to the same spot. And the spot is beautifully evocative, with a little forest walk, lakeside views, and a stirring inscription on the grave, drawn from Kleist's own work: "Now, immortality, you belong to me!" It is augmented by another memorial inscription, composed by Max Ring ("He lived, sang, and suffered in somber, difficult times, he sought death here and found immortality"), which—there always being a Jewish angle in these stories—was removed during the Nazi period, owing to the ethnic status of its author (we've already met him in Schönhauser Allee). What most gives this little sanctuary its sensation of presence, of exactly what was missing in all those Mitte addresses, is that the double suicide and the grave are in one and the same location; we are, in other words, in the presence of both the act and the persons. And the fact that it is Rahel's letter in which this event is first announced ("He is—and remains—a man of courage") places her once again in the defining center of a German cultural moment.

Elsewhere, of course, you can visit Rahel's own grave. A pair of simple ground level markers at a little distance from each other in the Dreifaltigkeit Cemetery and almost, but not quite, overgrown with ivy commemorates both Rahel and her husband. Behind them a display tablet bears words that she requested, according to Varnhagen, as her epitaph. Addressing the "Gute Menschen" who pass by her grave, she enjoins, "When something good happens for mankind, then, in your joy, hold me in remembrance as well." Stirring words; of course, you are reading them in the midst of a Protestant cemetery—the price, as it were, of her marriage to the man who reposes there next to her. You'll find many converts and their families nearby, the roster of names having many overlaps with those in Schönhauser Allee. Including, of course, Mendelssohn. In contrast to Rahel's simple stone in the ground, Fanny and Felix are each commemorated with a cross; given Felix's three Christian names and his double-barreled surname, it took quite a bit of lapidary ingenuity to make sure everything could be jammed into the cruciform shape. Overcompensation, perhaps?

In a similar vein, not far away you can find Henriette Herz, her information also etched on a cross, but of far more elaborate design, as sketched by the great German architect Karl Friedrich Schinkel. Converted to Protestantism (apparently Schleiermacher's doing) during her widowhood, she reposes alone, her husband already interred among the Jews in the Grosse Hamburger Straße graveyard, along with Moses Mendelssohn.

This talk of conversion raises some fundamental questions. Rahel was baptized at the age of forty-three, well into her years of prominence. How is it then that an unconverted Jew could find herself at the very hub of culture in Berlin, hobnobbing with Goethe and Beethoven, the Humboldts and the Schlegels, nobility and royalty, stars of both the musical and the lecture theater? Before one gets to that question, it's probably worth asking why it should *not* have been possible. The answer is that, as of the middle of the eighteenth century, Jews in all the territories that had once constituted the Holy Roman Empire had hardly seen much change in their status since the later Middle Ages. At times, they benefited either from the occasional enlightened local ruler or from their utility as bargaining chips in struggles between not so enlightened rulers. Still, for the most part the Jews in these regions had little freedom as regards where they lived, what kinds of work they could do, and whom they might associate with; their language was Yiddish (or, more precisely, Judendeutsch), not German, and their education was limited to sacred studies—which, as it happens, rendered them generally more educated, and certainly more literate, than Christians of an equivalent class.

For an index to the change, one might point to the Enlightenment (also the Jewish Enlightenment, called the *Haskalah*), as well as the occasionally well-disposed Frederick the Great of Prussia, whose policies led to a privileged condition for a delimited number of Jews in Berlin. This dispensation, which included Rahel's family, though they were far from the top of that small heap, may well signal the origins of that special relation between Berlin and Jews which lasted for nearly two centuries and, incidentally, is the premise of this book.

Within that story looms the pivotal figure of Moses Mendelssohn, especially as his fame was disseminated via his friend Gotthold Ephraim Lessing, who fictionalized him as the hero of *Nathan the Wise*. Still, we should not overlook that in 1743, just a generation prior to Rahel's birth, the teenage Mendelssohn found himself, part beggar and part yeshiva boy without a yeshiva, seeking entry to Berlin via a specially designated gate where Jews were allowed to petition for such entrance, and to pay for the privilege. Or—to observe anti-Semitism as theater of the absurd—we might recollect that when Mendelssohn got married, he was as a Jew obliged to spend a bundle of money on otherwise unsalable pieces of china from the Royal Factory. In his case, the white elephant was actually twenty porcelain monkeys, which remained in the possession of the family for many generations. Be that as it may, he was able to become a world famous philosopher, confidant of monarchs and fellow-geniuses.

It would be nice to say that between the beggar boy's appearance at the Rosenthaler gate and Rahel's investiture as the city's oracular tourist attraction history makes a big leap in a short time. It would be more accurate, though, to say that the culture in which Jewish and non-Jewish Germans cohabited during these decades was one of unending ambiguity and contradiction.

No surprise that among the Jews there were stark divisions in the lives of the rich vs. the poor, the western vs. the eastern, the secularized vs. the orthodox. But the fault lines of ambiguity within this culture run even deeper than those binaries. Emancipation was ambiguous because, to pick one example, the seemingly benevolent Act of Emancipation in 1812 made some things better for the Jews and other things worse—that is, it gave some of them citizenship but made all of them less autonomous. The profession of the intellectual was ambiguous because universities were neither entirely closed nor entirely open to Jews. The international scene was ambiguous because the liberalizing tendencies that came from the France of the Revolution and of Napoleon turned the Jews into potential Francophiles just when they needed, and wanted, to be patriotic Prussians. For similar reasons, armed conflict was ambiguous because, while it might offer an opportunity to exhibit Prussian patriotism, some Jews were thought to be unwilling to fight whereas others were thought to be war profiteers. Religious reform movements were ambiguous because, given their potential for bringing Jews into the modern world, they were opposed by an unlikely alliance between orthodox rabbis and the Prussian state apparatus, which was suspicious of upwardly mobile Jews who nevertheless wanted to remain Jews.

And, speaking of remaining Jews, religious reform was itself at mortal loggerheads with conversion, which was itself ambiguous because the transformation of Jews into Christians raised the question of whether one's identity qua Jew could be washed off at the baptismal font. In other words, what did it mean to be a Jew? That, after all, is the *big* question.

Nor did you have to be Jewish to live a life of contradiction around the Jewish question. Take the very much interwoven stories of three great philosophers within this culture. Hegel's dialectic view of history depended absolutely on the notion that Judaism had been superseded; on the other hand, he was a strong supporter of the rights of Jews to university positions without the necessary step of conversion, and his ties with Eduard Gans (among other Jews) brought him in close touch with the modern scientific study of Judaism. Schleiermacher, famously opposed to the rationalist Hegel and proponent of a romantic, not to say sentimental, Christianity, was nevertheless closely connected with many prominent Jews, both socially (e.g., Henriette Herz, Dorothea Veit Schlegel, and Rahel herself) and academically, in supporting August Neander (né David Mendel) for the chair in—of all things—theology at the University of Berlin, while at the same time supporting a group of anti-Jewish students at the same university. Fichte resigned as the University rector when a different group of anti-Jewish students were not expelled—the same Fichte, that is, who in the 1790s had declared that the only way Jews could be integrated was to decapitate them and replace their heads with Christian heads. It's also the same Fichte who managed to be ferociously nationalist in his wildly popular lectures under the title "Addresses to the German Nation" without emerging as anti-Semitic—a feat rarely achieved in later times. And both Fichte and Schleiermacher, whatever their potential for philo-Semitism, helped found the Christian-German Eating Club, conceived more or less explicitly as an antidote to the female and Jewish salons. But then, Rahel's husband Varnhagen was also involved in that undertaking.

Or, leaving the echt Christians behind, we might consider the lives and careers of two composers. Giacomo Meyerbeer—we met him in the bosom of his family at the Schönhauser Allee cemetery—kept the faith, though not the name. Having emerged from the very pinnacle of Berlin Jewish wealth and high culture and promoted by his stage mother Amalie Beer, he emigrates to Paris, and, while sending synagogue music back to Berlin, he writes *Les Huguenots*, about a group of persons who are in some sense a coded version of his own more persistently persecuted minority. No love lost between him and the much younger Felix Mendelssohn, of a convert family where there was also a name change, with "Bartholdy" floating in and out of the generations, depending on their attempts at Christian assimilation. Converted or not, Felix received a professional boost from one Karl Zelter, another Christian-German Eating Club member who— talk about contradictions!—wrote music for Reform services but also wrote to Goethe about the young Felix, "He is the son of a Jew but he is no Jew. . . . It really would be *eppes rores* [that rare thing—Zelter descends, appropriately, into Yiddish] if a Jew boy were to become an artist."

The last laugh belongs to that (converted) Jew boy, and it can stand as the capstone for all these interfaith intricacies. In March of 1829, Mendelssohn, having struggled with his mentor Zelter and against the prejudices occasioned by being rich, young, and amateur—among perhaps other prejudices emerging from the largely *Judenfrei* Berlin Singakademie—gets his way and conducts the previously neglected *St. Matthew Passion* of Johann Sebastian Bach. The performance created a sensation: Hegel, Schleiermacher, and the royal family are all in the audience, as is our own Rahel. *Eppes rores* has taken place: Mendelssohn has not only confirmed himself and J. S. Bach; he has placed his ancestrally Jewish hands upon the very pinnacle of Christian music.

Felix Mendelssohn offers an incomparable case study for Jewish Berlin, and Zelter's "commendation" of him as a Jew-but-not-a-Jew tells us everything we want to know about this multiple and contradictory civilization. The stories we are told about the emancipation of the Jews in nineteenth-century Germany often place conversion at the center. From my perspective—that is, in the relationship between Jews and culture—conversion is essentially meaningless. Marx is a Jewish political thinker even though his thoughts on "the Jewish Question" have been labeled anti-Semitic; Heine is a Jewish writer even though he ridiculed the social pretensions of his own people; Mendelssohn is a Jewish composer even though he earned fame with a celebrated performance of the *St. Matthew Passion*. They were all converted, but so far as the register of *culture* is concerned, they were all Jews. And Jews, indeed, they remain. Which, come to think of it, is why I felt so proud of myself when I put my ritual pebble on Felix Mendelssohn's cross-shaped grave stone: not in chastisement of him or his family, but as a gesture of welcome, honoring himself and myself at the same time.

And Rahel is a Jewish salonnière even though. . . . But there is a long list to complete this particular expression of *Paradoxie*. Even though she frequently and eloquently cursed her own ethnic identity. "It is so hateful to be a Jewess," she writes to her friend Regine Frohberg (herself a Jewess; one biographer notes that Rahel's girlfriends tended to be either Jews or noblewomen), though in this case the offense is merely that a well-meaning gentile automatically assumes from her religious background what her opinion of genius will be. (Namely, that it overrides all considerations of ethics; a Jew was apparently Nietzschean avant la lettre.)

Other frequently cited passages from her letters express the matter more passionately:

> I can never get it into my head that I am a Schlemihl and a Jewess, that even after all these years and after so much thinking about it, it has not dawned on me, I shall never grasp it. That is why "the sound of the executioner's axe does not gnaw upon my roots." That is why I am still living.

And:

> I imagine that just as I was being thrust into this world a supernatural being plunged a dagger into my heart, with these words: "Now, have feeling, see the world as only a few see it, be great and noble; nor can I deprive you of restless, incessant thought. But with one reservation: be a Jewess!" And now my whole life is one long bleeding.

Hannah Arendt takes outcries like these pretty straight and uses them to nail down charges that Rahel was fatally deluded by the promises of the Enlightenment.

That may be true, but when we take a closer look, we see a more complex tangle of beliefs and desires. The letter about being "ein Schlemihl und eine Jüdin," written in 1793, is an answer to Rahel's friend David Veit (a fellow Jew), who has recently been granted the privilege of visiting Goethe—a privilege not yet accorded to her—and it resonates with a sense of unentitlement, both on religious and gender grounds. It is also, however, steeped in an almost ostentatious mastery of Christian German culture. The quotation about the executioner's axe is drawn from Goethe's *Egmont*, near the moment of the hero's death (itself a religious issue, since he is a Dutch Protestant being executed by Spanish Catholics). So Rahel has the text of Goethe's (quite recently written) play at her fingertips, and she identifies with it. On the other hand, she identifies with it *negatively*, since in the original the executioner's axe *does* gnaw on his heart. On the third hand, the very focus on this passage—which turns up elsewhere in her letters—about cutting and not cutting is bound to arise from some of the most basic issues of difference between Jews and Christians. On top of which, the very phrase "ein Schlemihl und eine Jüdin" depends on a piece of Biblical-origin Yiddish that had been quite thoroughly domesticated into German. Domesticated, that is, without ceasing to be Jewish—which makes the person *Rahel* and the word *Schlemihl* partners indeed. If this is Jewish self-hatred (a detestable phrase and, for me, most applicable to those who accuse others of it), it is also an expression of pride. The same goes for Rahel's whole life as "one long bleeding." Along with the dagger in the heart, the "supernatural being" has bestowed upon her a golden array of "Jewish" traits: deep feeling, unique vision, continuous questioning, and a natural nobility that defies the world's petty categories of inherited social class.

Of course, all this philo-Judaism wrapped inside anti-Judaism as expressed by Rahel herself must come up against a far simpler and nastier account of the matter by those around her. However Rahel might strive either to escape from or redefine her identity, there were plenty who nailed her as a Jewess without any fancifying attributes—even among those close to her. One could consider ambivalent the remark by Kleist that "Jewish Society would be my favorite if the Jews did not act so pretentiously about their cultivation." It's harder to discount Ludwig Tieck's personal screed against Rahel that runs through her lack of artistic or poetic sensitivity, along with her tendency to jesuitical (!) argumentation, and culminates, "And can she please ever forget to play the Jewess? In the end, it's all about Jewish literature and placing that dissolute Heine, the Jewish Messiah, in some ways above Goethe." Among the inner circle, Caroline and Wilhelm von Humboldt exchange quite vicious accounts of Rahel, particularly centering on her marriage: Varnhagen, writes Wilhelm, "has now married the little Levi. Thus she is able now to become an ambassador's wife and an Excellency. There is not anything which cannot be achieved by a Jew." He didn't mean it in a good way.

Yet they chatted with Rahel, they visited her tea table, and, in the case of Caroline von Humboldt, they even used the *du* form mutually in correspondence with her. (The Humboldts, by the way, needn't have worried so much; after Rahel's marriage there were many high-end invitations extended to her husband but not to her.) If Clemens von Brentano was able to call the conversation chez Rahel "slovenly"—and he, along with his close friend Achim von Arnim, also tight with Rahel's circle, have many anti-Semitic credentials—it's because he was regularly on the premises. Whatever the cognitive dissonance involved, these titled Germans were forced to recognize that the cultivated salonnière and little Levi the Jewess were one and the same person.

That this was not necessarily an easy recognition emerges from a curious fact. The picture we have of life around Rahel has, ever since Varnhagen published her life and works in extenso, owed a great deal to four contemporary documents: the eyewitness accounts of an 1801 visit by the Austrian Count von Salm, and an anonymous visitor from 1830, followed by two extensive memorial tributes composed shortly after her death by the Marquis de la Custine and Gustave von Brinckmann. These remarkable chroniclers—whose accounts I have used liberally in these pages and whose novelistic talents I have celebrated—leave no stone unturned in describing Rahel herself, her surroundings, her conversation, her personality, and her relationships. One thing is missing: in some hundred fifty pages of exhaustive tribute, never once is it mentioned that she is a Jew.

Lest it seem unwise to argue *ex silentio*, from what *isn't* said, it might be pointed out that Karoline Bauer, whose highly vernacular account of Rahel contrasts across the board with what we hear from the aristocratic gentlemen, displays no such scruples on the religion front, several times mentioning Rahel's "sharp Jewish features," recollecting her own childhood fascination with Rahel's baptism at age forty, and recounting the life of Rahel's brother almost entirely by reference to the religion into which he was born, including a full transcription of his sonnet that begins, "If you're a Jew, who from the mother's womb | Has already been condemned to the status of a slave. . . ." Clearly, there is a connection between the high-class adulation of Rahel as Berlin's queen of companionability and the silencing of her identity as a Jew, some sort of pact to which Karoline Bauer was not a signatory.

Should we conclude from all this that, from the 1790s onward, when Rahel is building her reputation as a salonnière, it is a liability to be a Jew? Not so fast. Beginning in the period when this social form is being born, other persons in the salon business include (just to cite some names that tell their own story) Philippine Cohen, Sara Levy, Amalie Beer, Henriette Solmar (née Salomon), and, of course, Rahel's most significant predecessor and competitor, Henriette Herz. Things will change by the 1820s and 1830s, when noblewomen and even (gasp!) *men* get into the act. But at this formative moment, according to one historian, nine of the sixteen assemblages that came to be called salons were in the hands of Jewesses or recently converted Jewesses. One percent of the population conducts fifty-six percent of the salons.

If we put that together with the discreet omission concerning Rahel's religion, we confront perhaps the biggest *Paradoxie* of all. In the world of culture that accommodates, all at once, these philosophers and poets, politicians and musicians, military men and diplomats, socialites and gossips, it seems as though the Jew—more properly, the Jewess—is indispensable yet, through some sort of collective and silent agreement, qua Jew, invisible. Indispensable, as it turns out, for a new definition of culture, in which persons of talent and sophistication, irrespective of preexisting social categories, are thrown together. Modernity-as-exogamy, a mixing that hadn't previously existed. It's not only the minority or borderline status of the Jew that makes her indispensable, but also the fact that the Jew—*this* Jew, at any rate—is an articulately self-ironizing figure, as she bitterly described herself: "have feeling, see the world as only a few see it, be great and noble; nor can I deprive you of restless, incessant thought." If all of this adds up to, as she put it, "one long bleeding," it seems as though that blood nourished Berlin.

Why, then, is the Jewess rendered invisible? There are some simple answers, having to do with all those ambiguities and contradictions in the status of Jews in this place and time. Whatever the causes, though, the result brings us back to the central premise of this book. Karoline Bauer uses the J word to talk about a people, a religion, a race, a body type, old familiar stuff. The eloquent noblemen who frequent Rahel's salon and never mention that she is a Jew are responding to something for which they don't yet have a name (hence the silence): they are present at one of the birthplaces where the Jew is emerging as the definer of European culture. There are many bad reasons why Jews should be invisible. This, however, is one of the good reasons: not because they are nowhere, but because they are everywhere, or at least in all the best places.

4

People: James Simon

A few years ago, I had the privilege of joining a private tour of
the newly reopened Neues Museum on Berlin's Museum Island.
New may need some glossing here. Among the city's great cultural institutions are the Altes Museum, the Alte Nationalgalerie,
and the Neues Museum, all of which are in fact quite old, dating
respectively to 1830, 1861, and 1855. But the Neues Museum, as I
encountered it in 2009, was really the *neues* Neues Museum. The
bombings of November 1943 and February 1945 had left it barely
a shell, its grand staircase and its frescoes more or less obliterated. Whereas some of the other structures in the Museum Island
complex had been reconstituted through the efforts of the East
German government during the immediate postwar period—for
instance, the architectural jewel of the whole neighborhood, Karl
Friedrich Schinkel's Altes Museum—the Neues was left pretty
much a rotting hulk for almost sixty years. The reunification of
the city, some forward-looking civic consciousness, and a great
deal of public expenditure brought together this ever deteriorat-
ing structure with the visionary efforts of the brilliant British
architect, David Chipperfield. It was his completed work that we
were touring.

And the building, which had become *neu* indeed, made a powerful impression. Not that the work hadn't been controversial:
there was even a movement afoot to demote it from the UNESCO
list of World Heritage Sites because its nineteenth-century form
was thought to have been violated. Quite the contrary, it seemed
to me. Chipperfield managed to reconstruct and reinvent the
building's past while adopting a style of elegant architectural
neutrality for those parts of the construction that had disappeared without a trace. As a result, I felt I was walking through
multiple strata of living history, amounting to a particularly stylish version of what one feels everywhere in Berlin. More than

most "new" museums I know (so many of which are designed ostentatiously by pop star architects), this structure, with its own history of obliteration, seemed to merge with the objects it was meant to exhibit, themselves victims of a far longer stretch of ruin than that which had been visited upon Berlin.

On the other hand, as I went through one elegant and welcoming exhibition space after another, each with some architectural mix of *alt* and *neu*, I couldn't help feeling that the ancient objects on exhibit didn't always live up to their surroundings. Call me philistine, but I can take in only a certain number of prehistoric tomb gewgaws before I glaze over and start fixating on the prospects for really good poppyseed cake at the museum café—the kind served to me as a child when I visited elderly relatives in Brooklyn.

Then I entered a mysterious and selectively spotlighted circular chamber at the center of which, it turns out, is the city's single most famous art object. She is Berlin's answer to that heavily promoted citizen of Paris, the Mona Lisa, and with much the same sense of eros and mystery. Like all great art, the Nefertiti Bust is incalculably more impressive in the flesh than in the photos: the impossibly ductile neck, the creamy complexion, the fact that a person with one normal eye and one pupil-less eye doesn't look in the least bit freakish. Still, her installation played no small role in the magic. Amongst museum spaces where fifteen or twenty tiny totems could crowd each shelf of each vitrine inside each exhibition hall, here in this expansive abode Nefertiti reposed majestically alone.

Or almost alone. To her right another bust was exhibited (alas, no longer). Judging from the style—something realist, something impressionist, something cubist—he is about three and a half thousand years younger, but appearing considerably more aged. He was identified as JAMES SIMON KUNSTMÄZEN. I knew the name slightly, having met the industrialist, collector, and humanitarian at his final resting place in Schönhauser Allee. And *Mäzen*, I also knew, was derived from Maecenas, the superrich Roman who provided lavish financial backing for the poet Horace, among others. So: *James Simon, Patron of the Arts*. Fittingly, he was placed next to his most famous acquisition and gift; at that moment in twenty-first-century Berlin, it seems, the Egyptian queen had a Jewish roommate.

In short, another Zelig moment, of a Berlin Jew turning up where you might least expect him. Rahel Varnhagen proved ubiquitous in the cultural life of the city during the first decades of the nineteenth century. Now we turn to an individual whose benevolence spreads over broad stretches of the same terrain three-quarters of a century later. We'll be finding him across Berlin's museums far beyond Nefertiti, but, as we'll see, he is also woven through some pivotal moments of the city's history as a place where Jews and Christians engaged in the project of cohabiting in the modern world.

For instance: the date is 1914 and the context is some early efforts to bring not only Jews but also Jewish-funded higher education to Palestine. Chaim Weizmann, Father of the State of Israel, recounts in his autobiography a struggle concerning the Haifa Technical College, planned as one of the first steps in creating a University in the Jewish-reclaimed Holy Land. The debate is on one particular point that might seem a mere cultural nicety (not to Weizmann, who links the topic with the coming of World War I), namely, concerning the language of instruction at the proposed institution of higher learning.

At this moment, in the waning days of the Ottoman Empire, the fledgling Jewish institutions in Palestine sought the backing of European powers, especially the French, the German, and, to a lesser extent, the British. The Technical College was under German protection—not surprisingly, given the prestige of the Germans in scientific learning—and as such it answered in particular to the (decidedly gentile) German Secretary for Foreign Affairs, Artur Zimmermann, author of the eponymous telegram that would before long help precipitate the entry of the United States into the war.

The meeting to decide on the future language of the Technical College took place in Berlin. Describing the scene, decades later, after two world wars and the birth of the state of Israel, Weizmann recalls, "Ranged against us were James Simon, the Cotton King, and Paul Nathan, his right-hand man, directors of the *Hilfsverein* and the undisputed heads of German Jewry. They were the usual type of *Kaiser-Juden*, like Albert Ballin and Max Warburg, more German than the Germans, obsequious, super-patriotic, eagerly anticipating the wishes and plans of the masters of Germany." Weizmann is in particular outraged to learn that the German Foreign Secretary has an interest in the matter. "At this point I blew up and asked hotly: 'What the devil has Dr. Zimmermann got to do with *our* Technical College in Palestine?' I saw genuine grief and terror on the faces of the German Jews seated at the table." It's easy to read the future in these particular tea leaves: within weeks, Weizmann, who had recently become a British subject, and the "superpatriotic" James Simon would be on opposite sides of a devastating conflict.

The issue here, however, is not so much world politics as conflicting visions of what it meant to be a Jew in Europe at the beginning of the twentieth century. To the dedicated Zionist, it matters little that Hebrew had long been a sacred rather than a vernacular language and that its career as a spoken tongue was barely thirty years old. In fact, what really angers Weizmann is the idea of the Jew as a fully fledged and enthusiastic European citizen. His only way of framing such a condition is as enslavement to an alien gentile power. "Grief and terror" accompany any disobedience to that master, who dares to dictate how *we* should operate in *our* Technical College. Equally troubling to him, perhaps, is Simon's association with the *Hilfsverein*, which was spending a great deal of money helping to relocate Eastern European Jews not necessarily in the direction of Palestine but to places like North America, where they would in their turn become enthusiastic citizens in an ecumenical national entity, just as Simon was, or believed he was, in Germany.

Many readers today—and not only Zionists—would side with Weizmann. For others, all the hindsight we possess about the consequences of strident nationalism, whether in Berlin, Washington, or Jerusalem, may render it difficult to adjudicate between Weizmann and Simon. But not for me, at least from the perspective of this early twentieth-century moment and, especially, in the person of James Simon (1851–1932). Berliner, Cotton King, *Kunstmäzen*, and *Kaiserjude*: the many-sided story of that individual, and the trails it opens through Berlin today, is what I wish to tell here.

As regards Cotton King, it should be recalled that Simon shares his ultimate resting place with Arnhold the Coal King and Flatau the Hops King, Schönhauser Allee being a regular *Invalides* for Jewish industrialists. Simon came by his title of commercial royalty in the most time-honored fashion. His family hailed from the western edge of Pomerania, then Prussia, now Poland—about a hundred miles and (for some) a couple of generations from Berlin. His grandfather, Wolf Marcus, begins as a rag peddler in the countryside, then moves to the nearby town (Pyritz, now Pyrzyce), where he sets up a retail business in textiles. His elder son moves to a yet bigger town (Posen/Poznan), sets himself up as a tailor, and weds the rabbi's daughter, thus in time-honored fashion, marrying *up*. A subsequent exodus takes them to the veritable outskirts of the metropolis; finally in 1838, both of Wolf Markus's sons reach Berlin. Wandering Jews indeed: five different places of residence, each time with a new set of commercial arrangements, all in something like thirty years. If other Jews (say, my own forebears, who began only a few hundred miles farther east) hunkered down for another century or so in the shtetl rather than seeking their fortunes westward, one begins to see why.

That migration also takes the Simon family in relatively short order from the pushcart if not to the boardroom at least to considerable marketplace prominence. Almost immediately upon reaching Berlin, James's father Isaak and his uncle Louis, together with a partner, open a men's wear shop. Before long, the partner drops out, and the family firm, Gebrüder Simon, mutates from a purely retail establishment gradually into wholesale, production, and international distribution.

Why is it so often the *schmatte* business? Judging from the case of the Simon family, it's clear that at one point in history, clothing—especially second-hand clothing—was a perfect commodity for the peddler, purchasable and salable passim, easy to transport, and required by all. Then, at another point in history, commerce in dry goods on a larger scale is greatly benefited by those who possess broad sets of personal connections, for instance, among subpopulations with a history of interrelation, marital and otherwise; and this bonding could operate even more effectively when it extended beyond the boundaries of nations. Gebrüder Simon had it all: a network of coreligionists in similar occupations within Berlin plus global scope, including England (where young James spent some time in the milltown of Bradford) and, eventually, the Middle East.

But regarding the Simon family fortune, perhaps the most significant piece of internationalism strikes us closer to home, in the form of an inspired forecast about US politics. Gebrüder Simon looked into the seeds of time and saw both the American Civil War and the Yankee naval blockade of the Confederacy. Thus they spent a number of years stockpiling cotton from the South in advance of the war; as a result, for a considerable period they had something approaching a monopoly and were able to make fivefold profit. So in the end maybe it's not just endogamy or cosmopolitanism; maybe it's just that Jews are clever about money.

James's lifetime corresponds quite closely with the full arc of the family business. He was born too late to recall the shopkeeping days, and yet, later in life when he is offered and declines an honorific title (as frequently happened), he is quoted as responding, "Can you imagine a customer having to say to me, 'Your Excellency, can I please have a meter and a half of linen?'" Simon ran no retail business, and no "customer" ever wandered into his "shop"; yet, like many other wealthy Jews, he couldn't quite get the atavistic peddler out of his system. Peddler in any case he never was. James enters the trade quite early, and within a relatively short time he becomes the standard-bearer. The elder generation steps aside, and after a while his first cousin Eduard moves away from business affairs and toward affluent leisure and art collecting (Ghiberti, Botticelli, Bronzino, Tiepolo; then, when the money runs out, suicide—but we're getting ahead of ourselves).

Simon is the undisputed Cotton King, just as Weizmann called him, for some three decades, most of which represent a meteoric rise in capital. Between 1880 and 1914, the annual revenue doubled, reaching a height of something like fifty million marks, with six million in pure profit. According to one report, Simon's own personal income in 1911 reached 1,500,000 marks; multiply that by 6 to approximate an equivalent in modern buying power. He was, or so it was said, the sixth wealthiest man in Berlin.

This good fortune didn't stretch quite to the end of his life. Dying in 1932, Simon escaped (barely) the political horror of his epoch, but he failed to escape the economic horror. The first setback was World War I. His firm might have profiteered in the 1914–1918 period—many did, and after all, armies need lots of cotton for their uniforms—but, perhaps owing to prejudice against a Jewish firm (one may recall the Loewe family's "Jew Flints," which were accused of covert subversion in 1870), they did not have a good war. And no one had a good defeat, which was followed swiftly by the catastrophic early 1920s phenomenon of the mega-inflation, captured in those memorable photographs of wheelbarrows full of paper money needed to buy a loaf of bread. The inflation subsided, but not the downward spiral of credit and debt. By 1929 (the year that James's cousin Eduard took his own life), Gebrüder Simon was on its way to bankruptcy. The villa by the Tiergarten, where Simon and his wife (who died in 1921) had raised three children, was sold, and the elderly Simon downsized to a flat in the less prestigious neighborhood of Wilmersdorf. He was neither destitute nor forgotten: a chauffeur still drove him around in a fancy car, and on the occasion of his eightieth birthday, Kaiser Wilhelm, now in exile after the World War I defeat, sent special congratulations. But his days as "Cotton King" were over.

Those imperial congratulations, along with the funeral wreath that the exiled Kaiser provided a few months later, take us back to Weizmann's term *Kaiserjude*. More than a century afterward, it is a paradox almost impossible to decode. We have a monarch who was known to rant against "Antichrist Juda" and to ordain compulsory attendance at nightly readings from the works of arch-Aryan racist Houston Stewart Chamberlain while also spending several decades of his reign in close and frequent contact with a group of highly placed German Jews, among whom James Simon was prominent. Were men like Simon, or shipping magnate Albert Ballin, or banker Max Warburg being cunningly exploited? If so, for what purpose? Unlike the court Jews of a century earlier, they didn't represent any sort of financial underpinning for the monarchy. And what was in it for them? Simon, as has already been mentioned, refused titles. Indeed, the Kaiser was overheard saying to his Prime Minister, "Do you know James Simon? That's a man who isn't looking for medals or decorations; he does what he does for its own sake."

Within this group, it was frequently said that James Simon approached closest to being the monarch's friend. The first time they met they spent an hour and a half together, both of them completely losing track of the time, or so Simon seems to have recounted to his housekeeper, to which she adds that the Kaiser treated him like an older brother. One occasion, when Wilhelm accepted Simon's invitation to visit the Fasanenstraße synagogue, gave rise to a much quoted exchange. The Kaiser asks Simon what his subjects are likely to think about his interest in Jewish matters, to which Simon replies in a daring moment of facetiousness, "Perhaps the rabbis will imagine that you're thinking about converting," with which His Imperial Majesty plays along by responding, "I hadn't thought the gentlemen were raising their expectations quite so high." The Slivovitz must have been flowing freely that night because during the same visit—the year is 1912, and the air is thick with war talk—the Kaiser gets loose-lipped about recent developments in regard to one of his closest allies. "If I hadn't held the Austrians back," he confides to Simon while exploring the shul, "those rascals would have embroiled us in war."

It wasn't all, or even mostly, about wars and religion. As witness another meeting of the two men. The year is 1904, and Simon's collection of Renaissance Art, which has been displayed in his own home, is soon to be donated in toto to the Kaiser Friedrich Museum. Wilhelm gets wind of this and decides on the spur of the moment to pay a call at Tiergartenstraße so as to have the pleasure of touring the collection in situ, at the right hand of the collector himself, before the whole thing is transferred to public view. The Kaiser—famous among his staff for his sudden whims—gets the idea at 8:30 A.M. and determines that he shall be accompanied by Simon through the collection at precisely 11:00 A.M. Herr Simon is not immediately available. He has, with his accustomed punctuality, already left for the office; in fact, he is currently in a meeting at the Reichsbank. Luckily, we are already in the age of the telephone: numbers are dialed, strings are pulled, and Simon is released from his important business meeting on grounds of imperial urgency. He arrives at home, with twenty minutes to spare—just enough time, apparently, to change from business attire to whatever one wears when the Emperor drops in—and is able to lead Wilhelm, admiring piece after piece, through several rooms of painting and sculpture.

"No one could spend time with James Simon without learning something": so the Kaiser is quoted as saying. And it's clear that, whatever his other excellences, he was at his most irresistible in his role as a collector. Wilhelm might learn about shipping from Ballin or finances from Warburg; from James Simon he learned about art.

It's time for another of those statistics about numbers of Jews. We have already seen how at the end of the eighteenth century, when their percentage in Berlin's population was infinitesimal, the majority of the salons were run by Jewish women. I recall as well learning (from one of those city-wide memorial exhibitions about the horrors of the past, this one entitled "Diversity Destroyed") that at a moment when 4% of Berliners were Jewish, the proportion of Jewish doctors at the prestigious Charité Hospital and elsewhere in the city was 50%. In both these cases, and many others, part of the story is that these enterprises were open to Jews, whereas others were not. Women like Henriette Herz or Rahel Varnhagen, besides suffering under the limitations placed on all women, were excluded from becoming, say, society doyennes in the ambit of the royal court, so they found openings elsewhere; a hundred years later, Jewish men became doctors in part because they couldn't so readily become judges or generals. Along with medicine, it seems, art collecting was at the beginning of the twentieth century something of a Jewish industry.

Putting this statistical matter another way, if instead of read-

ing the tombstones in Schönhauser Allee, we were to find ourselves in the household art collections of those who are interred
there, we might choose to admire the Italian Renaissance Sculpture collection of Louis Süssman-Hellborn, or the immense range
of Buddhist art from India, Indochina, Tibet, and Japan on display chez Gerson Simon (no relation of James's), or the Courbet
and the Renoir in the home of Carl Hagen, or Rubens's *Bound
Slave* chez Markus Kappel. Alternatively, if you merely visited
the immediate neighborhood of James Simon himself in Tiergartenstraße, you might take in the eclectic selection of painting, prints, and arts and crafts at No. 4 (Valentine Weisbach),
or the Chinese Collection at No. 8d (Oscar Wassermann), or the
Byzantine and Venetian glass at 18e (Hermann Rosenberg), or
Brueghel's *Alchemist*, along with a wide selection of medieval
wooden sculpture, at 8a (Benoit Oppenheim). You really couldn't
swing a cat in the right Berlin neighborhood without clawing at
a Jewish art collection.

James Simon wasn't the wealthiest Jewish collector, nor did
he own the largest number of masterpieces. But he managed to
amass works of art in radically different genres, media, time peri-
ods, and geographies. He began quite early with something of
a buying spree in Dutch still lifes. It was a good place to start.
These works were not particularly fashionable in the 1880s, which
kept their prices down. They were colorful, uncomplicated, non-
sectarian (not that he would always avoid sacred subjects), and,
once the Tiergartenstraße house was suitably arranged, they
functioned beautifully as dining room decoration.

A considerable rise in collectorly ambition, starting at a relatively early moment, landed Simon squarely in the Italian Renaissance. In Florence he picked up a *Salome with the Head of John
the Baptist*, attributed to Fiorenzo di Lorenzo, while in Paris he
acquired the *Portrait of a Young Man* that has now been assigned
to Giovanni Bellini. A portrait, a biblical scene; an Umbrian, a
Venetian: if this seems a bit scattershot, it's because Italy was a
difficult market to break into.

Undaunted, Simon branched out toward media involving less
competition, including Della Robbia ceramics and Renaissance
Italian statuary in bronze, wood, and clay. All of which testifies,

once again, to a well-cultivated frugality in assembling beautiful things on a budget. But the real coup confirming his status
as ingenious man of taste, lover of the Renaissance, and perspi-
cacious bargain hunter was the acquisition of an extraordinary
assemblage of bronze medals. These works—essentially, miniature two-sided sculptures often designed by major artists—
represent a fascinating entry point not only to the art but also
to the whole culture of the period. And they could be had at a
good price, as we learn from an 1889 letter in which Simon pon-
ders whether he should bargain down a collection of 340 pieces
from 30,000 to 25,000 marks, or whether he should wait until
the collection was broken down for the auction so that he could
cherry-pick the best of them.

Medals may stand as a kind of symptom of Simon's attraction
to the so-called "minor arts" and to the Italian Renaissance. But
some of his most important areas of acquisition pointed elsewhere. Georg Haberland, it will be recalled, found expression for
his Jewish soul by memorializing Bavaria, the Rhineland, and
Richard Wagner in the neighborhoods he built. James Simon,
surrounding himself with works on the domestic scale, collected
Germany. By no means was high art excluded, even if no maker's name could be attached, as witness his exquisite assemblage
of small sixteenth-century polychrome figures from Bavaria or
the Rhine. But he showed equal enthusiasm for the objects of
German daily life in that same idealized past. He collected door
knockers, pastry molds, nutcrackers, tin soldiers; he financed a
half-visionary, half-kitschy project to create miniature houses
representing the building styles among different regions of the
nation. Not only did he have a decidedly forward-looking aesthetic appreciation for the objects of daily life; it's also clear that
he had a thing for tchotchkes.

In all this assemblage of stuff, from Renaissance painting to
kitchen tools, Simon did not work alone. After all, in roughly
the same period American robber barons like Mellon, Morgan,
and Frick were following the dictates of such aesthetic experts
as Bernard Berenson. The comparison is more than an intellectual exercise. Berlin in these years was becoming a city of wealth,
high culture, and centralized world power in exact parallel to a

number of American cities. The competition was inevitable, and in no arena more savage than art collecting. Suffice it to point out that a 1911 German volume entitled *The Psychology of Art Collecting* devotes an entire chapter to what it calls *die Amerikanische Gefahr*. The American threat, it turns out, is none other than J. P. Morgan, whose massive entry into the art market is bringing on a meteoric rise in prices.

Simon's Berenson is Wilhelm von Bode. (In America the gentile millionaire has a Jewish advisor; in Berlin, the Jewish millionaire has a gentile advisor. A matter worth pondering.) Bode had risen from assistant curator of sculpture in the Berlin Museums, beginning in his twenties, to head of department to director of the Gemäldegalerie to general director of the Berlin Museums. When the two men first met, Simon was an obvious neophyte, but Bode clearly recognized in him the makings of a great pupil, someone who would translate the master's judgments into substantial purchases.

In the early days, that choice of Dutch still lifes was engineered by Bode, who clearly saw these genre pieces as both pretty and pretty cheap. But by the time Simon had become head of the family firm, thus blessed with deeper pockets, the stakes were higher, and the conversations concerning issues of expertise and issues of cash become more heated. Bode likes a certain Frans Snyders, Simon doesn't care for it; Bode proposes a Canaletto, Simon says it's too expensive. Bode gives his nod to a Rembrandt, Simon buys it but insists on keeping its high cost a secret. And as for the Mantegna now in the Gemäldegalerie, Simon has his heart set on it and buys it despite Bode's objection that it is overpriced.

In all this give-and-take, it's important to Simon that he is a man of taste as well as of wealth. Clearly, he wanted to distinguish himself from some imagined common run of rich culture-hoarding Jewish collectors like his neighbor Markus Kappel, who wrote to Bode, "Under no circumstances will I buy anything without taking your wisdom into account." Simon, on the other hand, directly communicates his pique, for instance, at what was a highly complimentary account of their collaboration that Bode published in 1905 because it left the impression that all Simon did was to put up the money. He ends by reminding Bode in no uncertain terms, "You know that I became a collector wholeheartedly and out of my own inclinations, not just for outward show."

It's an intense relationship, including moments of close collaboration. The acquisition of the Mantegna, for instance, occasions a major re-hanging of the collection, and there is a flood of requests for Bode's advice: the color of the walls, the distance between paintings and windows, the appropriate choice of tapestries, the suitable surroundings for the display of medals. On the other hand, like all relations between teachers and their brightest students, it was volatile. It wasn't just that Simon wanted to express his own preferences as regards the work of canonical artists; he also began to collect well outside Bode's interests or even his expertise. Anonymously crafted wood sculpture and used kitchen equipment were not Bode's idea of art, and these enterprises pulled the two men apart.

Then, too, there were underlying matters that had little to do with art. At this distance, and even with dozens of extant letters between the two men, it is difficult to gauge whether the bond between them could meet any sort of test for friendship. Perhaps it was difficult for Simon himself. At a certain moment, Bode, who was widowed quite early, expresses a wish to marry again, and Simon—what can he have been thinking?—recommends his own niece, Dora Lesser, of whom, he says, "your daughter could never have a more tender or understanding second mother." The silence in response is deafening. It becomes clear that the gap between a Simon (or a Lesser) and a von Bode was at certain fundamental levels unbridgeable. Indeed, when Simon began definitively to collect on his own, Bode wrote to his friend, the archaeologist Theodor Wiegand—who died in 1936 but not before signing the manifesto of "German Scholars Supporting Adolf Hitler"—that, looking at Simon's collection of antiquities, you could tell he was nothing but a *Großkaufmann* (punning on both "wholesale" and "gross"). Just a bigger version of that shopkeeper who has to be addressed as "Your Excellency" when you come to buy some dry goods off him.

But, as in so many other instances, it would be wrong to view the Bode-Simon relation exclusively via hindsight. When Simon writes on the occasion of Bode's retirement, "Working alongside you belongs among the most valuable experiences that life has brought me," or when Bode writes that during a period when everything in Germany was falling apart (referring to the World War and the inflation that followed upon it), Simon was a beacon of light, both keeping his collection together and generously donating it despite his own family's hardships, these are not formulaic sentiments. Rather they are a sign of a culture in collaboration: private and public, money and taste, gentiles and Jews.

Donating is the key word. None of this would have taken place as it did, if Bode had been merely an art advisor. Both the intimacy and the complexity of the relationship depended on the fact that Bode was the most powerful figure in the German museum world, closely allied with Kaiser Wilhelm in the project of making Berlin a center of world art. To accomplish his task, he needed not only rich collectors but also those who were willing to donate their collections to the public. Bernard Berenson, it may be recalled, was straddling between the art market and the collector; Bode, for his part, was straddling between the art market and the museum through the intermediary of the collector. Each case has its own whiff of corruptibility, and there are moments when it's apparent that Bode is coaxing Simon into a purchase for the sake of a future museum gift. When Simon, for instance, demurs in the purchase of some unidentified Renaissance painting, declaring that he doesn't want the work for his collection, Bode replies, "That's not the question. The Museum requires it. We can't let it go, and we can't afford to purchase it on our own. In time, you'll learn to appreciate it." Simon bought the picture.

But that glimpse of a power play ought not to distract from the magnitude of Simon's initiative as a person who, year after year, decade after decade, handed over artworks that he had purchased for his own collection to a whole range of Berlin museums, which were being founded in this period and built up with the Simon donations at their center. Whether or not Simon was (as he occasionally feared) Bode's mere tool in assembling the collection, he nevertheless took the lead aggressively, and beyond anything Bode could dream of manipulating, in the way he dispersed it.

A catalogue of donations to the Prussian museums during this period enumerates the gifts of seventy-eight Jewish benefactors. (How remarkable, by the way, that there *were* seventy-eight Jewish benefactors!) Most of these lists take up a page or a page and a half; a handful take up two pages. James Simon's list of donations covers fifteen pages.

The first major transfer, which took place in 1904 at the opening of the Kaiser Friedrich Museum, consisted of almost 500 pieces: 29 paintings, 19 large sculptures, 48 smaller works in three dimensions, 388 medals, and a selection of objects in ivory, wax, and metal, with a bit of Majolica thrown in. The second big move from Simon's personal gallery to public display occurred in 1920 with the inauguration of the Deutsches Museum. This donation consisted of some 350 pieces, notably a major assemblage of German and other Northern European works in wood, along with some of the arts and crafts that were becoming dear to Simon the collector (and less dear to Bode). It was a moment, what with the defeat in World War I and the strains on the German economy, of far greater personal sacrifice than was represented by Simon's generosity sixteen years earlier; all the more remarkable that this collection was valued at over two million pre-inflation marks.

The flood of individual donations from Simon's personal holdings preceded these mega-gifts and continued thereafter. Collections of Italian bronzes as early as the 1880s, coins and miscellaneous paintings (including a Courbet) in the 1890s, folk art and collaborative gifts of Asian works after the turn of the century. Not to mention the gift of cash—some half a million marks to the various museums over the years. What it all adds up to is that however distinguished James Simon was as a *collector*, he was even more spectacular as a *donor*.

All of this, and we haven't come anywhere near that Nefertiti head in front of whom I first met Simon face-to-face. In fact, what may have been his most important acts of art-related generosity were of quite a different kind from all these transfers of his personal collection to the state. Indeed it is difficult to imagine two more dissimilar enterprises than those which yielded Mantegna, on the one hand, and Nefertiti, on the other. In one case, a gentleman visits a few galleries, attends the odd auction, and satisfies his own private aesthetic by committing to some judicious purchases; in the other case, that gentleman is playing a managerial role on the world stage.

Archaeology, it turns out, is nothing less than a lightning rod for all the most explosive aspects of European culture during the decades leading up to World War I. The territories that stretched from Syria and Palestine across Mesopotamia and into Egypt were capturing worldwide attention, and the historical markers that lay under their virgin soil were (literally) up for grabs. And the same sort of power vacuum—that is, a weak and decentralized Ottoman rule—that allowed Chaim Weizmann and his collaborators to be constructing a Jewish technical college among Muslim populations offered opportunities for all kinds of cultural imperialism out of the West.

Germany was in a particularly volatile position. Academically, it was the great center of classical philology. But everything about Germany's Johnny-come-lately status among world powers threatened to be replicated by the fact that England and France had also managed to take the lead in undertaking archaeological expeditions. Germany, after all, had already flunked the project of mounting an overseas empire; now it seemed fated to be, once again, left out. In response, Kaiser Wilhelm, famous for his exploitation of cultural objects as sources of power, responds superpatriotically to the challenge of the French and the English enjoying a monopoly on excavations. A leading archaeologist puts the battle cry succinctly: "Prussia must dig!"

Simon dug. He helped support the earliest public initiative (called the Orient-Kommittee) until he came to realize that it was undercapitalized and lacking in a broad base of supporters. He became a founding member of the Deutsche Orient Gesellschaft (DOG), which exists to this day, where, thanks to him, the vastly increased membership brought together academic experts, museum leaders, and individuals with close ties to power. Within a short time, it became the best-funded entity in the world devoted to archaeological enterprises in the Near East.

Not only did Simon know how to run a business, he also had a genius for public relations. Annual reports (still being issued today), rewriting of archaeological jargon into language the public could understand, help from his publisher friend Rudolf Mosse (neighbor ultimately in Schönhauser Allee) with placements in the popular press: Simon arranged it all.

Publicity was, however, only part of the undertaking; one had to get the right central actors involved. As a good *Kaiserjude*, Simon knew where to start. Everyone knew that Wilhelm was a highly interested party, but Simon took the lead in exploiting this resource. That first meeting of the two (about which his housekeeper recalled that both men lost track of the time) was largely devoted to upping the Kaiser's interest in the DOG, and Simon knew well enough to enlist the monarch's closest advisor, Admiral Friedrich von Hollman, thus creating an ongoing symbiosis between Prussia's international policies and the interests of those excavating in the East.

Simon also knew how to find the right people to do the actual work in the field. He established a fruitful partnership with Robert Koldewey, who, more than anyone else, would institute the modern layer-by-layer method of archaeology, as opposed to the bulldozer-style top-to-bottom excavations that had previously been the norm. It was Simon who had the foresight to hire him and to persist uncomplainingly through the beginning stages of the stratigraphic method, which inevitably start by yielding very little to justify the enormous expense. (They needn't have worried: by the mid-1920s, hundreds of crates of objects were being shipped to Berlin.)

And the expense was enormous, with Simon always tending the treasury. Once Kaiser Wilhelm became the official protector of the DOG—again, owing in part to Simon's efforts—money flowed in unabated. The royal purse itself contributed over four hundred thousand marks, and the Prussian treasury almost two million. Besides his involvement in procuring these bits of largesse, between 1897 and 1918 Simon himself threw in almost half a million from his own pocket.

Hundreds of hours, loads of money: what can explain the magnetism of this undertaking for a man who during these same years was operating as the boss of a huge commercial empire? We know he was a good German, but there is more to this than nationalism. Back in the 1880s, in one of the first ventures of this kind undertaken by the Berlin Museums, a modest expedition was mounted for the purpose of ruin-hunting in the hills of Mesopotamia. The whole thing was funded, to the tune of 30,000 marks, by a single benefactor: Louis Simon, James's uncle. A few years later, an opportunity arose to purchase a highly significant collection of clay tablets from Tell el-Amarna (prophetically, the region where the Nefertiti would be found decades later). Once again, the price was around 30,000 marks. This time, however, the patron was Isaak Simon, James's father. Neither of these men was a grand patron of the arts, like their son and nephew: Near Eastern archaeology, in other words, seems to have been a special case.

One more indicator, this time from James himself, concerning his early interests and education. The slim pickings in the search for autobiographical writings from Simon (how different from Rahel, who wrote thousands of letters about herself!) consist of two brief and rather stilted reminiscences, the first composed when he was eighteen and the second when he was fifty-nine. The teenager freely confesses a whole lot of scholarly ineptitude, for instance, in both grade school arithmetic and high school math, nor is he a whiz at modern languages. On the other hand, he is gripped by Latin and Greek, "especially once the works of the ancients were gradually made available to me," and he goes on to say that in the higher grades he felt increasingly the desire to be a scholar, to work in philology, though "certain significant obstacles lay in the way of that discipline as a life work." Forty years later, he is quite explicit about the obstacles: "I felt myself most attracted to the study of ancient languages and history, but that inclination was not so strong that I could overcome my father's wishes for me, as an only son, to become a partner in the business." It's worth noting that his weak points—French, English, Math—were exactly what would serve him well in the future that he was being obliged to pursue. Philology not so much.

His answer was to work out multiple futures, bringing his business skills up to speed while also indulging in his passions for the ancients. But *which* ancients? Like others of an intellectual bent, Simon learned Latin and Greek in school, not Hittite or hieroglyphics. Indeed, mainstream study of the ancient world, which reached one of its pinnacles in that very nineteenth-century German philology that so tempted young James, was always focused on the West—the premise being that Athens and Rome represented the origins of *our* civilization. But who exactly are *we*? Some of us trace our lineage firmly to the ancients, but not necessarily to those who spoke Greek and Latin.

So, if Louis and Isaak, with no credentials in classical philology and no art collections, invested in enterprises to unearth materials from Mesopotamia and Egypt, it's reasonable to conclude that they felt they were getting closer to something of their own origins—rather than, say, collecting manuscripts of Virgil or portraits of the saints. Of course, to connect the Simons comfortably with Mesopotamia and Egypt, we must unlearn the history in which Arabs and Jews are mortal enemies. Louis and Isaak and James, in other words, are all recognizing that in the stretch between the Euphrates and the Nile they are finding roots. Of course, like any form of "racial" thinking, it can go quite sour. The proposition that there was a common heritage of Semitic peoples also contributes to the fantasy of the "Aryan" race.

But the magic of archaeology in the Near East is that it needn't be divisively sectarian. The digs in Mesopotamia yield thousands of tablets in cuneiform, ancestor of *all* Western writing systems; and discoveries in the kingdom of Utnapishtim provide new grounding for the epic of Gilgamesh, which reveals its close connections to the story of Noah. Excavations on the site of Babylon—the name itself carries biblical magic—gave rise to a publicity blitz surrounding an idea promoted by Assyriologist Franz Delitzsch that many stories in the Hebrew Bible had Babylonian origins (again, a premise fraught with the potential for racism). Whether one believed this claim or not, the *Babel-Bibel Controversy*, as it was called, generated enormous attention for the archaeological project. Delitzsch went on to yet larger and more vastly syncretic assertions that the Babylonian temple of Esagila revealed itself as the original of the Greco-Roman pantheon. If Babylon, now that it was being excavated, could be understood to be *every* culture's property, Egypt was even more so. It was, after all, prime biblical land; and, via Akhenaten, a source of monotheism, as witness the widespread idea articulated by Freud and made famous during this period that Moses was Egyptian. We are, in short, in the homeland of the Bible; and, as for those exploring a personal heritage that fits more seamlessly with Homer and Pericles, Cicero and Caesar, than with Moses, we are in the homeland of their origins' origins.

Then there was Palestine. It can't be a pure coincidence that some of Simon's colleagues in the DOG—including Delitzsch of the Babylonian origins of the Bible—were cool toward excavations in the region. Nor should it come as a surprise that Simon, as a result, took personal charge, for the first time paying for the whole enterprise out of his own pocket. The first efforts unearthed early synagogues in Galilee, though the excavators had to fight with some of the locals, who wanted to bulldoze the ruins in order to make houses for Jewish colonists (*plus ça change...*). The focus then turned to Jericho, enabling the excavators to begin unearthing layer upon layer through several millennia. Not only does Simon continue to foot the bill, but he emerges from the shadows when diplomacy is necessary. When the money stream for Jericho threatens to dry up and the excavator-in-chief finds himself at odds with the DOG back home, Simon holds a private peace conference in his own Tiergartenstraße residence. Simon's diffidence throughout his philanthropic career in putting himself forward, from whatever combination of shyness and selflessness, seems to melt away with these undertakings in the Holy Land.

The experience of Galilee and Jericho places Simon in a kind of starring role that reaches its pinnacle once the archaeological projects move to Egypt and, in particular, Tell el-Amarna. Whether for ethnic reasons or not, Simon clearly nourishes a passion for Egypt. It is Simon who secures the Kaiser's involvement on the international scene, since Egypt had been a French and English archaeological monopoly up until then. He dispenses yet more of his own funds, so that it's possible for the first time to undertake digs in more than one place, an enterprise that involves six hundred workers (three or four times the usual size of the team). By 1911, when the focus has moved to Tell el-Amarna, the responsibility shifts entirely to Simon: he signs the excavation request, and it is under his name, not that of the DOG, that the treasures are collected. As a result—and this is unprecedented—the German share in the discoveries becomes his private property. That is a circumstance to which we shall return.

Simon's expenditures in both art and archaeology, it turns out, had their limits. When, for instance, he turns down a painting by Francesco Guardi, or when he goes art-shopping to Rome but ends up buying nothing, the reason he reports to Bode is that he is completely strapped for cash: "I have been so deeply engaged in private and public giving this year, already well into the thousands, that I have to impose limits on myself for the rest of the year." He wasn't just poor-mouthing. The truth of the matter is that, however much Simon spent on art, in both money and energy, he spent even more on charity.

The stimulus for his extraordinary career in civic benefaction lay around him in all the Dickensian social woes of the nineteenth-century city. No surprise, then, that Simon's focus is on the health, well-being, and education of the most disempowered urban dwellers, as is clear from the names of some of the dozens of organizations he supports: Association of Girls' Shelters, Berlin Association for Public Baths, Home Health Care Society, Society for the Protection of Children from Exploitation and Abuse. One of his most energetic involvements is the project of creating summer vacation opportunities in the country for boys and girls. Another, the Association for Public Entertainment in Berlin, mounts a vast program of low-cost cultural activities under the banner of "Noble Companionability and Educational Stimulation, Especially through Musical, Declamatory, and Edifying Presentations." "Companionability," or *Geselligkeit*, is exactly what Rahel Varnhagen's privileged intimates were celebrating in her company; a century later, the generosity of James Simon and his kind has the ambition of producing trickle-down. His investments in social clubs, hospitals, and old people's housing reached something like two hundred thousand marks, and the project of summer getaway homes probably ran even higher than that. By one account (that of the Berlin Police, who took note of these things), he gave away a quarter of a million marks per year for a couple of decades; another estimate tallies something between a third and a quarter of his total income. No wonder he had to economize a bit on Italian paintings.

If this list of charities is ethnically unaligned (some might use the term *goyish*), it is also the case that Simon, like many others in his community, was actively involved in a thriving network of specifically Jewish charities. Among these, Simon supported aid organizations concerned with the indigent, with Eastern Europeans who were studying in Germany, and with young girls, also from the East, who were victims of immigration scams that turned out to be—in the quaint language of the time—white slavery.

But the real center of Simon's money and energies in this area was the Hilfsverein der Deutschen Juden. Around the turn of the century, a number of events in Eastern Europe placed Jewish suffering vividly before Western eyes, including a series of pogroms within the Pale of Settlement and the imposition of further restrictions on the already limited civil rights of Jews in Romania. Circumstances like these produced a widespread project of emigration to which the assimilated, bourgeois, and prosperous Jews of the West responded with large-scale charitable undertakings. Within a few decades, the French, the English, and the Austrians had created their own organizations; in Germany, the crises gave rise to the Hilfsverein, for which James Simon served as president for over thirty years—indeed, for almost the entire time the organization existed.

Even today, controversy surrounds this enterprise. The Hilfsverein, with Simon's help and expertise, raised something approaching a hundred million marks over its lifetime, and it spent its money on indubitably worthy projects, notably the improvement of educational facilities wherever disadvantaged Jews resided and—even more significantly, at least for my own family story—the support for Jews who wished to escape the tribulations of life in the East. (One of its presumably lower-budget undertakings was a per diem support of emigrants who

Gallery 2

Figure 3.1

Rahel, with her famously penetrating stare, surrounded by some of the faithful. From left to right: Ernst von Pfuel, Heinrich von Kleist, Frederike Unzelmann; Dorothea Schlegel, Karl August Varnhagen von Ense; Friedrich Gentz, Prince Louis Ferdinand, Karoline Bauer.

Figure 3.2
Nothing is left of Rahel's first salon in her parents' attic room at Jägerstraße 54 except a plaque, but a glimpse into the elegant, and heavily gated, inner courtyard offers a sense of Berlin's residential intimacy. Photograph by Nick Barberio.

Figure 3.3
The location of Rahel's second salon, where she entertained luminaries of the younger generation in the 1820s. As with most of these sites, nothing remains; in this case, though, there are some touristical memories of premodern transport. Photograph by Nick Barberio.

Figure 3.4
The unusually well preserved home of philosopher Friedrich Schleiermacher, sometime disciple and sometime critic of Rahel's hospitality; aloft nearby, the helium balloon that advertises Berlin's *Die Welt* newspaper and offers fifteen minute rides to today's tourists. Photograph by Nick Barberio.

Figure 3.5
From one salon to another. Where Rahel's contemporary and competitor, Henriette Herz, once consorted with artistic and literary luminaries, Berliners can now avail themselves of the latest tanning equipment. Photograph by Nick Barberio.

Figure 4.1
A lost painting by Ernst Oppler (1904) depicts James Simon in his study surrounded by works from his collection, which were about to be transferred to the Kaiser Friedrich Museum; the man himself stares distractedly beyond the objects in his collection.

Figure 4.2
Gallery 39 in the Kaiser Friedrich Museum as photographed ca. 1904; the works have been transferred directly from James Simon's home, and they are installed so as to recreate something like their original domestic setting. Photo: bpk, Berlin / Staatliche Museen, Berlin / Art Resource, NY.

Figure 4.3
Fifty-year-old James Simon at his desk, as painted by Willi Döring; in the darkness one can recognize items from his collection. As in the Oppler painting (Figure 4.1), he gazes not at the art works but into the distance. Photo: bpk, Berlin / Staatliche Museen, Berlin / Art Resource, NY.

Figure 4.4
The installation of Queen Nefertiti is the pièce de resistance of David Chipperfield's redesigned Neues Museum; for a while, this same majestic space also housed a bust of the donor, James Simon. Photo: bpk, Berlin / Neues Museum, Staatliche Museen, Berlin / Art Resource, NY.

Figure 4.5
The supreme jewel of Simon's painting collection, Vermeer's *Mistress and Maid*, which he acquired in 1905 and sold to Henry Clay Frick in 1919. It was one of the very few works that Simon converted into cash rather than giving to the people of Berlin. By way of the Frick Collection, it now belongs to New York. Photo: Copyright The Frick Collection.

Figure 5.1
Walter Benjamin was photographed in Paris by Gisele Freund, who, as it happens, grew up in the same Bavarian Quarter building where Einstein lived. © IMEC, Fonds MCC / CNAC / MNAM / Dist. RMN-Grand Palais / Gisele Freund / Art Resource, NY.

Figure 5.2
The Kaiser Panorama, a public access stereopticon that fascinated young Walter Benjamin, can still be enjoyed today in the Märkisches Museum; then as now, it generally exhibits scenes from the long ago or the far away. Photograph by Nick Barberio.

Figure 5.3
Walter Benjamin longed to capture a feather on his enthusiastically anticipated childhood journeys to Berlin's Peacock Island; not much has changed there since 1900, but this young girl has had better luck than little Walter did. Photograph by Nick Barberio.

Figure 5.4
Potsdamer Brücke over the Landwehr Canal as it is today, but with an old-fashioned life preserver such as inspired some of Walter Benjamin's melancholy musings as he recollected his childhood wanderings in the neighborhood. Photograph by Nick Barberio.

Figure 5.5
Can this be the same city that was so memorably photographed in 1945 as an expanse of debris? It's not difficult to find stretches of the city as gracious as those where Benjamin walked, though his mother would probably not have allowed him to wander as far from home as these handsome structures along the canal in Kreuzberg. Photograph by Nick Barberio.

Figure 6.1
The grand public space just off Kurfürstendamm designed and named in honor of Walter Benjamin; whether these are the kind of arcades that he would have approved of remains an open question. Photograph by Nick Barberio.

Figure 6.2
The commemoration of Rahel is located at an urban crossroads, but rather far from her sphere of influence and in a style that she might not find congenial. Photograph by Nick Barberio.

Figure 6.3
The *Stolperstein*, or stumbling stone, that I encountered every day in front of my door in Goltz-straße. Frau Scherl lived in the building and operated a furniture store there. Her life (along with all the others commemorated in the *Stolpersteine*) has been meticulously reconstructed; see http://www.stolpersteine-berlin.de/de/biografie/3452.

Figure 6.4
The quietest memorial of all: Grunewald's Track 17 commemorates the spot where, day after day, Berlin's Jews were shipped eastward. Photograph by Nick Barberio.

were passing through Germany on their way to the West. I take this very personally: my mother's dimly recalled childhood experience of walking on Unter den Linden, circa 1907, which she often recounted to me, may well have been subventioned by a bit of James Simon's cotton money.)

The trouble was that the flourishing of this highly praiseworthy enterprise coincides with some of the most virulent battles both within and beyond world Jewry as to the geography, the language, and the politics of that grand project of migration over which they were strewing their benevolence. The Hilfsverein was clearly enthusiastic about rescuing Jews in the direction of North America, for instance teaming up with Jacob Schiff in encouraging Galveston, Texas, as a port of entry, a project that was supposed to relieve the pressure on the Northeast United States and to discourage the overcrowding of urban ghettoes—such as, once again, my own family in their Henry Street cold-water tenement knew all too well.

Did this set of initiatives make the Hilfsverein anti-Zionist? Weizmann seems to have thought so. Insisting that the language of instruction at the Haifa Technikum be German amounted to a betrayal: the repurposing of Hebrew from the language of the Bible and of ritual into a working modern vernacular was, after all, a cornerstone of *Eretz Israel*, the biblical land fully restored to modern Jews. But Weizmann doesn't tell the whole story. The Technikum was coming into being largely because the Hilfsverein was paying for it. Not only might this give them (and not Artur Zimmermann) some rights in deciding what went on in the college, it also demonstrates that the Hilfsverein was indeed investing heavily in Palestine on behalf of a Jewish future there—*cultural* Zionism at the very least—and not just spending all its money on shipping *Ostjuden* off to the Lone Star State.

The truth of the matter is that these decades represent a moment when the future of Eastern European Jews is not only fearful but also facing a wildly open-ended range of utopian (not to say crackpot) possibilities. On the one hand pogroms, on another hand philanthropists, on a third hand Palestine, on a fourth hand a plethora of proposed homelands including Uganda,

Madagascar, British Guyana, and remote parts of Argentina or Australia. It is no wonder that these years witness a stormy series of World Zionist Congresses and that compassionate and generously philanthropic Jews are calling each other nasty names. So what else is new?

James Simon is at the center of these quandaries: so what kind of Jew is he? The kind who collects Pietàs, who spends millions on Berlin's gentile, as well as Jewish, poor, who is riveted by the artwork of the Egyptians, and who is branded by the first president of the state of Israel as a German toady. Even his engagement in Jewish charities seems to have always been on behalf of the needy, not on behalf of the torah. We know he escorted the Kaiser to the Synagogue, but there is not much evidence that he often visited without royalty in tow.

Before we consign him to excommunication, two glimpses of Simon-as-Jew, the first from his archaeology days, the second from the War. One of the most productive areas of excavation at the turn of the century had been the village of Bogazköy in central Turkey, where thousands of cuneiform tablets were being unearthed and the history of the Hittite empire was being made manifest. The archaeologist in charge was Hugo Winckler, and, when it was determined in 1907 that quite a lot of money was needed, the sponsors turned immediately to the two men who had been the most generous donors to all these undertakings, one of whom was James Simon. The problem was that Hugo Winckler was a dedicated anti-Semite, the most fervent exponent of the hypothesis concerning the Babylonian origins of the Bible; and it was he who made the most explicit claims that these origins demonstrated the inferiority of the Hebrews.

When approached for financial support on this dig, Simon responded that he would be happy to contribute if, *and only if*, Winckler came to his house and explained what he needed the money for. This was virtually a unique stipulation in the history of Simon's archaeological benefactions; it was indeed a cornerstone of his philanthropy that he sought little personal recognition and disliked expressions of gratitude. The interview was brief. "How much do you need?" "30,000 marks." Simon, smiling, took out his pen and wrote a check for the sum requested; transaction complete. As for the other anticipated benefactor, it was none other than Kaiser Wilhelm. The Emperor's donation was neither more nor less than Simon's: 30,000 marks.

A few years later, the world has changed, and James Simon is being asked to play in a higher-stakes game. It is an early moment in the World War, and there are significant neutral nations, not the least of which is the United States. One of the central organizations for French Jews issued a public pronouncement that the Jews of the world should oppose the German side in the hostilities owing to Germany's history of anti-Semitism. (Never mind France's own sorry record in this regard. *Dreyfus, schmeyfus*: this is war!) Once again, James Simon unto the breach: that same Secretary-of-State, Artur Zimmermann, of the battle over the Haifa Technikum, urged that this appeal be answered with a vigorous defense of the Fatherland's record as a hospitable place for its Jewish citizens.

Simon is less obliging than he was with Winckler and far more independent than Weizmann made him out to be. In an elegantly written letter to Zimmermann, he declines to mount the requested defense, declaring that in a short time the whole thing will be forgotten. But he goes much further, questioning whether the French claims about the sorry situation of Jews in Germany are indeed erroneous:

> It is a fact that while the German Constitution provides for equal rights to the Jews, they are to this day denied access to the Civil Service, to the career of an army officer, tenure of a professorial chair, active service as military doctors, etc., not to mention further details. This is well known to the French and to the Russians. Our endeavors to ameliorate the lot of the Russian Jews have always been countered on the Russian side by the advice that we should protest first of all against the prejudicial treatment of the Jews on the part of the Prussian government. A reply by the German Jews to the appeal of the *Consistoire central* would stir up all these things and would be a political defeat.

A little masterpiece. Simon evades the objectionable task not out of philo-Semitism but on grounds of national self-interest:

if I were to write this reply, Mr. Secretary, Germany would end up looking bad. He further intimates that Germany's standing among nations suffers from its treatment of the Jews. And, most direct of all, he cites crucial areas of inequality that the constitutional protections have done nothing to remove—this last assertion concluded with the portentous suggestion that there are plenty more such signs of anti-Semitism that he, not to mention Germany's wartime enemies, could enumerate at will. Not quite the terrorized groveler of Weizmann's recollection.

What kind of Jew was James Simon? Bourgeois, liberal, statesmanly, global, supremely generous in giving but bashful in accepting thanks. If we think of him today, we should think of him as a man with a taste for art that was as eclectic as it was unerring, also as a man who gave more than half of his wealth to charity—and that half in equal proportions between liberal causes improving the lives of Berlin citizens and the donation of his art to the city, which was, in fact, *also* a liberal cause improving the lives of Berlin citizens. If my preference among all Berlin Jews is unashamedly James Simon, it is first of all for this familiar mix of prosperity, civic responsibility, and passionate love for art, all of which leaves its mark on Berlin in the twenty-first century.

If we are to look for that mark today, we must engage in a kind of treasure hunt for the objects that he sought after, purchased, unearthed, exhibited, and ultimately gave away. Many important works will elude us in this treasure hunt, having disappeared; others will have made their way through the horrors into twenty-first century Berlin just as they were when they first caught his eye.

One of those casualties is a painting by Ernst Oppler of James Simon in his private study (Figure 4.1). We have a photograph of the painting and a photograph of the study from the same angle, though minus Simon himself. Putting all this together, we can see the man within the intimate space of his collection before any of the wholesale dispersals that were to enrich Berlin's public collections had left the building. Conforming to the taste of the time, no space in the study is left unadorned. A wall with a dozen paintings in close proximity; a desk with a fairly casual assortment of figurines; a couple of display cases tightly packed with medallions; a fireplace mantle crowded with miniature bronzes overshadowed by an expansive clay portrait bust. It must have been barely possible to navigate the room, let alone to enjoy the spatial possibilities for display that important artworks might be said to command. No matter: the painting locates Simon at his desk, cheek by jowl with the objects, but with his back to most of them. In fact, he is looking off into the remote distance beyond the picture, and beyond the art.

The placement gives us a Simon who is less a collector than a work of art himself, that effect achieved because the wall behind the collector, against which his own portrait finds itself, is a study in human facial character. A chubby-cheeked dark-bearded young man, probably Venetian sixteenth century, is turned slightly to the left and looking out at us. Bronzino's portrait of another young man is fingering some sort of arithmetic book but more interested in directing his cool stare far off in our direction. An even more restrained figure, of an elaborately coiffed young woman, with a geometrically perfect décolletage, gazes to her left and pays the viewer no mind at all. Yet another young man, with a striking haircut and a handsome gown of his own, balances her with a gaze toward his right. At eye-level in the middle of the wall, the Mantegna Virgin and Child, one wakeful and the other sleeping, are wholly absorbed in themselves and connected to each other via the gentlest of touches. On a side wall, an ever so slightly grinning young Renaissance boy-cardinal, in painted clay, stares out at nothing. Nothing grandiose in size or conception; everything concentrating on the intimacy of human expression.

Much of this room is completely unrecapturable. The building is long gone. The art had been moved to a specially dedicated set of exhibition spaces in the Kaiser Friedrich Museum (Figure 4.2)—the signal honor of such an installation, and the (unfulfillable) promise that it would remain as it was for a hundred years, seems to have produced resentment for at least one of Simon's anti-Semitic fellow collectors—but no surprise that this museum-within-a-museum was shut down and Simon's name expunged after 1933. Then, after the war, when museums began to reopen, not everything remained extant, including the most striking object on the study wall in the painting and the photograph, a *tondo* more than a meter in diameter, attributed by some to Filippino Lippi, depicting the Adoration of the Christ Child. Installed for safe keeping in an impregnable anti-aircraft tower, it perished, somewhat suspiciously, in a fire that broke out several days *after* the fall of Berlin. In this fate, it joined some 416 other meticulously inventoried paintings, including works by Rubens, Andrea del Sarto, and, my special favorite, the Caravaggio *St. Matthew and the Angel*, which three centuries earlier had suffered the indignity of being rejected by the priests who commissioned it, thus being demoted from icon to collectible.

So the domestic scene in which Simon displayed his work is gone, as are the faux-domestic scenes inside the Kaiser Friedrich Museum and the Deutsches Museum. Nor, in contemporary times, was a decision made to reconstruct, as well as possible, the Simon rooms as they were in either museum. For what it's worth, I approve. James Simon's largesse extended to the whole of the city, and I am happy to travel, and to urge others to travel, in an experience of hunting them down among Berlin's gracious museum spaces. You may have the good fortune of seeing some of his Asian art—for instance, work by Utamaro and by Shunshō in Dahlem's Museum für Asiatische Kunst; and some of the German domestic items, including the model of a winemaker's cottage, are often on display in the nearby Museum für Europäische Kulturen. And you will certainly not want to miss the Ishtar Gate at the Pergamon Museum. Though it wasn't a James Simon collectible, its presence is owing to the generosity and enterprise he showed in underwriting so much of the Babylonian excavations and bringing them to Berlin as their second home.

But if you are making the James Simon pilgrimage and, as it were, repairing the damage done by the 1930s decision to remove all the museum labels reading "Gift of James Simon," there are certain places where you will find his taste most conspicuously on view. You can board the city's excellent transport system and catch the Mantegna and the Bronzino alive and well in the Gemäldegalerie, along with such other Simon donations as the Bellini portrait of a young man and a married couple rendered in a pendant pair of small-sized likenesses by the sixteenth-century German painter Bartholomäus Bruyn—all of which demonstrate that same focus on human character in the face that clearly excited the collector.

But to feel yourself most deeply in the presence of James Simon's art, you must head eastward from the Gemäldegalerie to the Bode, where so much of his art had once been on public display and is now once more. It's appropriate to begin with the James Simon Room on the second floor (if you can find it), which includes a portrait from 1901 (more of which anon), some biography, one of his Della Robbia glazed terra cottas, and, as elsewhere in the Bode, some remnants of severely damaged objects that record the effects of war on the Museum's collections.

Fanning out from this rather meager shrine quite soon, you'll discover James Simon everywhere. If you're tireless, you may get to see as many as eighty works of art whose labels include his name ("Geschenk James Simon," "Sammlung James Simon," or variants thereof). You'll be disappointed if you're looking for world-famous masterpieces, though you have my permission to renounce Simon just long enough to stand speechless in front of the Donatello Pazzi Madonna. Returning to the Simon scavenger hunt, you'll see some relatively large-scale objects, for instance, two very different representations of Calvary, both with myriad figures in something between two and three dimensions. Look at these crowded works closely, and you'll see that they are made up of exquisite miniatures. When I stare at these dozens of flawless little forms, I'm always reminded that among Simon's donations, in addition to artworks, was his collection of 140 toy soldiers. (Alas, nowhere on view, so far as I can determine.)

The miniature in all its forms is everywhere in Simon's Bode. There are, for instance, two irresistible tiny banquets, a fifteenth-century Last Supper in alabaster—note the sleeping Peter, diminutive even by the scale of the other figures—and a sixteenth-century Spanish Marriage at Cana in walnut, with the hostess's exquisitely minuscule hands smoothing out the table cloth. Don't miss the fifteenth-century Holy Kinship (a briefly fashionable religious subject based on the legend that St. Anne, the Virgin's mother, was married three times and bore three Marys—

who knew?), in which four saints, eight babies, and ten miniature grown-ups are characterized individually and yet form part of a beautifully integrated design: look for the little guy with the Phrygian cap whose arms reach slightly outside his pictorial space. And then there are the individual portrait figures, also presented in little: a reliquary box takes the form of a juvenile Virgin Mary, and a keenly focused, fashionably attired sixteenth-century gent who catches your gaze with his (love his seventies 'stache!). Neither of these is more than eight inches high.

All these human figures in small form may help us understand why Simon was such an avid collector of Madonna and Child sculpture (I counted ten such recently, outdistancing any other iconographic subject). Not so much the Virgin Mary—after all, he appears to have had no special weakness for Catholicism—as the portrait of the Child. That would explain the attractions, both for him and for us, of some of the most arresting of his works in the Bode. Two completely different sixteenth-century St. Christophers feature the saint and the child in powerful conjunction. In one of them, the carrying of the baby is a feat of acrobatics; the other is all serenity: Christopher holds the child, and the child holds the globe of the world. In both cases, the focus is on the child.

As it is elsewhere among the Simon donations. Looking at *St. Vitus in a Kettle*, one forgets the gruesome story of the saint proving his Christian faith as he is tortured by being half immersed in a cauldron of boiling pitch. Instead we see a graceful but slightly bizarre man-child, a little bit rouged and with flowing blond locks, whose slender body morphs halfway down into a great big garnet pot. One final lad, St. Crispian. The virtuoso carving of hair and garments arrests the gaze, but what really summons the viewer is Crispian's own absorption. The saint's backstory, prior to the usual grisly martyrdom, is all about his pious and meticulous labor as a cobbler. Here, though minus his right hand, he is intent on his task of shaping the shoe that has been belted on to his left leg. Be sure to go around the back, where you can take careful note of his fifteenth-century lunch basket.

Making this Bode-Simon pilgrimage, it is not hard to see the appeal of early modern domestic-sized wooden sculpture. These are artifacts of intimacy, of labor, of childhood, with all the heroics of religious suffering and awe reconceived in petite human scale. It is no wonder that this extended family should find a haven in James Simon's home spaces; they all find their own kind of communion with the viewer. All personal reminiscences of James Simon include the recollection that he loved children. We can share that love in the Museum today.

Returning to the memorial room in the Bode where we began, we find that second portrait of Simon in his private gallery, this one fortunately still in existence (Figure 4.3). Painted by Willi Döring a few years earlier than the Oppler portrait, it nevertheless directs us toward later phases of his engagement with the arts. The conception is very similar: the man is surrounded by his collection, but his gaze bypasses the objects and settles in a remote contemplative space. Simon is himself framed by a densely packed selection of the artworks that adorned his study up until he donated them to the Kaiser Friedrich Museum, among which we can glimpse the married couple from the Gemäldegalerie, the Andrea Pisano Madonna and Child from the Bode (perhaps; after all, he collected so many of them), and a Netherlandish polyptych of saints recorded in the Museum gift but no longer to be found. Himself a bit like the Bronzino boy, Simon fingers what may be important papers—the work on his desk that he is supposed to be doing—but his mind is elsewhere.

I believe I know where his mind is wandering as he stares out the window: he is thinking of Egypt. After all, the thin beam that illuminates the room also draws attention to one of the most spectacular Egyptian objects whose presence in Berlin is due to James Simon. The so-called *Berlin Green Head*—represented by Döring as wholly dissimilar from the paintings on the wall and staged in a more prominent position—is an arrestingly powerful bust of an old man. Though we encounter the ancient object here in Döring's portrait, the place to find the real thing, along with many other of the most evocative examples of both his taste and his generosity, returns us to the Neues Museum, where I first met Simon.

The project of Near Eastern archaeology, as I've already suggested, was an enterprise of vast global scope, as demanding for James Simon as the management of a business empire. But that gesture of distraction from the desk in the Döring portrait and the proximity of the spectacular Egyptian artifact on the desk remind us of something in Simon's version of archaeology that is far more intimate than global. Simon did indeed fund expeditions from Mesopotamia to Egypt, both in conjunction with other patrons and as a board member of the Deutsch-Orient Gesellschaft. But he also did something rather more anomalous, and more private: he received news from his network of archaeologist collaborators of specially significant *objets*, particularly in Egypt, and he plunked down the cash to *buy* them.

The Green Head, priced at £2000, was acquired by Simon in 1894 at the suggestion of archaeologist Adolf Erman; ten years later, it was a telegram from Ludwig Borchardt that induced Simon to purchase the portrait bust of Queen Teje. A graceful little wooden figure of a robed monarch has always been known simply as the *Simon'sche Holzfigur*; and by the time that the extraordinary sculpture workshop of Thutmose was unearthed, including the Nefertiti, the archaeological project was so thoroughly under the single leadership (and purse) of James Simon that he was, by some combination of de facto and de jure, the owner of the objects unearthed.

No question that these objects were ultimately destined for the Berlin Museum Collection of Egyptian Art. But that *Green Head* on Simon's desk reminds us that James Simon the patron of archaeology was never very far from James Simon the art collector, different as those enterprises might have been in their origins. If the brilliantly executed contemporary style of Chipperfield's Neues Museum takes us far from their installation in Simon's private space as rendered in the Döring portrait (as well as far from Egypt), it is nevertheless valuable to return the man to the works, if only in our imagination. If we wish to meet James Simon at the Neues Museum, and not just find ancient Egypt there, our attention should focus—as it did among the Renaissance paintings in his study, as it does among the wood sculptures in the Bode—on his taste as a collector for the intimate representation of the human form. It is, after all, just at this early twentieth-century moment that art historians are beginning to understand how the lifelike rendering of human beings, thought to have begun with the Greeks, actually originated in Egypt. In effect, James Simon is travelling back in time from Italian Renaissance painting to late medieval wood sculpture to the originators of human representation a couple of millennia earlier.

The *Green Head* is mesmerizing not only for its iridescent material and its uncanny modernity but most of all for the haunting solemnity, almost reproachfulness, of its demeanor. Queen Teje fixes her gaze on the viewer, or perhaps just above the viewer's head, with a kind of quizzical restraint, as though hesitating a bit wearily to impart some wisdom drawn from long experience. Pharaoh Amenhotep, with the high crown of Egypt seeming to grow straight out of his head, has the clenched jaw of an individual hardened by the exercise of authority. Quite a different impression radiates from a limestone bust of the young Akhenaten. Whether we accept Thomas Mann's lengthy character sketch of this figure as all about decadence—the haughty and fatigued character of an overbred young Englishman, weak chin, languorous eyelids that never fully open, sickly roseate color of the full lips—or we see something a little less febrile, Akhenaten certainly emerges as a fellow human, a personal ancestor, rather than a hieratic idealization.

All of these persons were the domestic companions of James Simon, but Nefertiti most of all (Figure 4.4). *Die bunte Königin*— the many-colored Queen—did not travel out of Egypt with the rest of the goods whose excavation Simon funded, even the best of them such as are now on view at the Neues Museum. She arrived earlier and by some kind of secret express service whose details remain unclear, which in fact complicates the questions of rightful citizenship that have hovered around her from that moment on. Simon, celebrated for his high ethical standards as a public man, may have never revealed those qualities more loftily than in his strong urging, a few years later, that she be returned to Egypt. (The meteoric rise of German chauvinism, ca. 1930, prevented any such repatriation.) The many-colored queen had not gone directly to the Museum; she was taken to Simon's house, where she reposed for several months. The rest of the Amarna discoveries were the subject of a gala private exhibition at the Berlin Egyptian Museum; Nefertiti, on the other hand, was visited in Tiergartenstraße in private by Kaiser Wilhelm. It is as if one central strand of Simon's passion for the arts—the capacity for communion between a modern soul and an ancient one, one face to another—is fulfilled in this extraordinary figure.

In his latter days, James Simon occupies a different milieu with a decidedly altered collection. Judging from a photograph of one room inside his Bundesallee apartment, there is no mistaking the scaled-down proportions of the domestic space; the room is of no very grand size, and the furniture, if Renaissance at all, is decidedly faux. He is not living without art, however. On a credenza, he has carefully arrayed a row of Egyptian figurines and heads; in pride of place at the center and dominating the rest—the others possibly scaled down in *hommage*—sits Nefertiti. They are all copies, of course; Simon had long since given up title to his Egyptian collection. But they are exhibited directly in front of different art: a pair of massive portraits, not the sixteenth-century married couple from the Gemäldegalerie, but Adolphine and Isaak, James Simon's parents. It's hard not to read this display as an autobiography. Less than forty years separate Isaak Simon's funding of a modest Egyptian expedition from the unearthing, acquisition, donation, and reproduction of Nefertiti, all at the behest of his son. In the interim, the artistic culture, along with many aspects of the public culture, of Berlin has been grandly enriched by the same individual.

It would be a mistake to conclude from this picture that James Simon remained in his final years with nothing but family portraits and a few copies from works acquired in the glory days. We possess a handsomely produced auction catalogue from November of 1932, six months after his death, reflecting a range of his tastes: painted miniatures, small-scale sculpture, household objects. Particularly notable is the collection of ancient jewelry and a few of the big-name paintings. Simon's friend Max Friedländer writes a sweet elegiac by way of introduction to the catalogue. Anticipating that the most valuable items in the auction are likely to end up exported to countries with stronger currency, he declares that the great age of philanthropy on behalf of Berlin's museums was, as he calls it, an "episode," which came to an end in 1914. "What Dr. Simon left behind," Friedländer writes, "strikes one as modest, in comparison with what he gave away in his lifetime. . . . On the whole, it represents a set of belongings, which apart from being of consistently high intrinsic value, is distinguished by the fact that Dr. Simon, in his years of prudent forbearance and seclusion, took pleasure in them."

Friedländer strikes exactly the right note: it should be clear from any visit to the great breadth of Simon's gifts across Berlin that his own personal pleasure was, more than any other impulse, at the center of his love for art. As witness two final works, which cannot be observed in any representation of Simon's house, nor do they turn up among his gifts. While it's true that even when financial collapse was closing in on him Simon continued to make notable donations, he also did some selling during those last lean years. There was an auction of several hundred lots in Amsterdam in 1927, including a very good Rubens (*Virgin, Child, and St. John*, present whereabouts unknown) and a haunting, if indecipherable, allegory by El Greco, now hanging in the National Gallery of Scotland. More lucratively, he raised a gigantic sum (around 800,000 marks, which were used in part to rescue his company's pension plan) in 1919 with the sale of his two greatest paintings, one to Andrew Mellon and the other to Henry Clay Frick: *die Amerikanische Gefahr* indeed!

Looking at Frans Hals's *Portrait of an Elderly Lady* and at Vermeer's *Mistress and Maid* (Figure 4.5), it is sad to think that Simon was able to hold on to these extraordinary works for a relatively short time, and that he could not take pleasure in them—indeed, in the vast majority of his astonishing holdings—during his "years of prudent forbearance and seclusion." On the other hand, when I look at them, having immersed myself in the life of James Simon as the Jewish magnate, aesthete, philanthropist, and *Kaiserjude*, I recognize the stamp of his personal taste. The beauty of human expressiveness, as with the Bronzino boy, or the shoemaker Crispian, or the Egyptian queen Nefertiti, shines through here as well, in the enigmatic facial rapport between Vermeer's mistress and maid and in the sly ironic grin of Hals's old lady.

And I *can* look at them. The Vermeer found its way to the Frick Collection, and the Hals to the Washington National Gallery. It is a tribute to James Simon that he bestowed his own pleasure not only across Berlin but also to the world.

By the time you read this, you may have the pleasure of another grand construction by David Chipperfield, a massive entry portico to the structures on Museum Island. It is to be known as the James Simon Gallery, in recognition of the many works in those museums which would not be there if it weren't for him. A grand tribute, though it puts me in mind of the sign that some clever Yale professor is supposed to have posted on the outside of the grandiose Sterling Library building when it was first opened in 1931: "This is not the library, the library is inside." The Chipperfield gallery is not the monument to James Simon, his monument is inside.

5

People: **Walter Benjamin**

Attention, Berlin sightseers! Admittedly, with the case of Rahel Varnhagen, it was just possible, and only with aggressive massage of early nineteenth-century data, to construct a little urban excursion around the locations of her famous friends. And as for James Simon, all that is left of him—though arguably the best of him—is the works from his collection that can be strategically tracked around the city. But now we come to an individual who actually composed his very own companion guide to Berlin. It's of a special kind, of course, and in order to follow its steps through the city, we need to take several paces back.

The estate sale of James Simon's remaining property, at which one might acquire anything from a Rubens Madonna (knocked down at 11,000 RM) to a pair of silk pillows (30 RM), was conducted by one of the preeminent disposers of such properties in Berlin, Rudolph Lepke's Kunst-Auction-Haus. The firm has a story like many others of its kind: its origins were sufficiently Jewish that it underwent "aryanization" after 1933, whereupon it began to be a clearing house for art pillaged from that legion of Jewish collectors whom we heard about in the previous chapter. Well before that time, however, and indeed before the James Simon auction, one of the leading partners in the firm was a certain Emil Benjamin. Emil sold his share in the company at considerable profit (though he apparently retained his personal auction gavel), realizing a sum of money that enabled him to invest in a broader range of enterprises, not all of which had the high culture cachet of Old Master paintings—for instance, a skating rink/dance hall, at which his habitually horny teenaged son remembered gazing longingly on a prostitute in a tight-fitting sailor suit. Be that as it may, the very comfortable economic conditions in which Walter Benjamin (Figure 5.1) was raised might be traced back to the Fine Arts.

If I belabor this tenuous connection, it's not merely to make the transition from Simon to Benjamin appear seamless. Consider the larger arc of our three Berlin Jews. Rahel Varnhagen is a figure, one might say, of pure high culture; commerce scarcely enters her story, her family having just sufficiently comfortable means to provide her with an entry ticket to a society over which she then achieved a conquest owing not to cash but to personality and sophistication. James Simon, on the other hand, is a preeminent figure of Jewish capital, whose fortune enables him to enrich his city's civilization immeasurably. With Benjamin, we return to culture tout court: he was, after all, incapable of earning a living or supporting his family, let alone of amassing wealth, whereas, to look on the positive side, his circle of friends, admirers, and collaborators provides a glittering portrait of creative intelligentsia in the early twentieth century much the way Varnhagen's did in the early nineteenth. But the real message to be drawn from this arc of personages is that Jewish Berlin depended on a kind of ignition between money and taste, whether those qualities appear in the same or in successive generations. Emil Benjamin creates a family fortune via a cross between High Art and commerce; and even though he eventually exchanges the sale room for the dance hall (and the medical supply business and the wine business), he enables his son to become, in time (though not exactly in his *own* time), a culture hero beyond the wildest dreams of Varnhagen and her circle.

Not that these three individuals fit comfortably together in all respects. Rahel Varnhagen, however deserving of twenty-first century attention, has had few turns in the cultural spotlight. James Simon, though currently being monumentalized inside a few square blocks of Berlin, generally provokes stares of nonrecognition, even sometimes in Berlin, when I say I am researching him. Walter Benjamin, on the other hand, has been elevated to the status of something like modernity's messiah, with the contents of hundreds of library shelves to prove it.

As it happens, Walter Benjamin's fame is one of the most interesting things—a skeptic might say *the* most interesting thing— about him, pointing toward a particularly distinctive life (and afterlife) narrative. Born into the upper middle echelons of Ber-

lin commercial money and status about forty years after James
Simon but with nothing like that level of wealth or social connection, Benjamin was freed, as Simon was not, to make the
choice of intellectual pursuits rather than family business. He
made that choice, one might say, with a vengeance, but even in
the academic business he was not a thundering success, at least
during his lifetime.

The roster of Benjamin's professional shortfalls is in fact rather
impressive. In his student days, he emerged as an up-and-coming
radical reformer but quit the movement when he was bumped
from the top job, and he never worked in politics again. As an
academic-in-training, he wavered between literature and philosophy and for years went from university to university without finding a whole-heartedly supportive mentor. He accomplished the doctorate with some distinction, but his attempts
at the *Habilitation*, which would result in a permanent teaching
job, were strikingly unsuccessful. His publication record—I speak
as a decades-long expert in evaluating such matters, albeit in
another age and another country—was, even during the period
when he was most prolific, fair to middling at best. He worked
hard on the founding of three different journals, but none of them
saw a single issue in print; and as for book publication, he produced one single ambitious scholarly tome and, other than that,
a couple of collections of personal vignettes that would (again
adopting my unashamedly anachronistic perspective) hardly
catch the notice of any tenure committee. Both of the projects
that might have qualified as his magnum opus remained fragmentary, one consisting of many disconnected pages, the other
of rather few pages, but likewise disconnected. To which one is
obliged to add the misadventures of his personal life: failed marriage, faulty fathering, tormented love affairs, drug experiments,
radical Wanderlust, both freely undertaken and forced upon him,
financial debacles, and, of course, the unutterable sadness of his
suicide.

An unfair account to be sure. It is accurate, perhaps, as an
assessment of his accomplishments from the perspective of 1940,
when he died, but not from the work that subsequent decades
have brought to light—hence, in part, the meteoric rise in his

reputation. However spotty the publication record, Benjamin's assiduousness in putting pen to paper (not, in this case, a metaphor, since he avoided the typewriter and fetishized the fountain pen) is astonishing. There seems to have been no moment in his tumultuous existence, however agonized his professional life, his love life, his political life, or even his life as a Jew-on-the-run, in which the troubles were so absorbing that he couldn't produce written text in small, medium, or large formats that posterity has found valuable.

The extraordinary range of these productions is doubtless partly a result of his turbulent biography, but it testifies even more to the grand scope of his talents, as well as to his unshakable faith in the written word. He wrote challenging works of literary criticism and radio plays for children; he wrote "pure" philosophy and travel ephemera; he did abstruse comparative theology and poetic close reading. Equally impressive is the way that he seems to have pre-written the subsequent half century of criticism, indeed of cultural work in general. He was theorizing literary Marxism before Frederick Jameson, appreciating the grit of urban clutter before Jane Jacobs, devoting serious intellectual attention to popular media before the Frankfurt School was called the Frankfurt School, doing linguistic deconstruction before Jacques Derrida, delving into the mythology of ordinary objects before Roland Barthes.

Truth to tell, I come to Benjamin as something other than an acolyte, having been made a bit uncomfortable by his status as guru and—more seriously—by a sensation when I read him that he is sometimes exchanging rigorous thinking for impressionistic eloquence. If I love him anyway, it is because I see this haze of language as a sign that he was perpetually yearning for the advent of truths that don't quite arrive or don't nestle comfortably with other truths. He lived, after all, at a peak moment when totalizing systems held their most absolute and effective sway. Religion, whether as theology or as racialism, had lost little of its power, while fascism and communism were, with violent if intermittent success, playing themselves out as all-encompassing unified field theories for arranging politics and thought. Walter

Benjamin lived in that world and in some respects embodied it, but I would argue that the jaggedness of his life and work can be traced to a refusal (tacit or even unconscious) to totalize. The sources of this refusal may well have to do with his admirable susceptibility to aesthetic pleasure or his love for the wayward qualities of poetic language. For me, though, it's the fact of being a Berlin Jew. Varnhagen's *Paradoxie*, Simon's concurrent mastery of international cotton, the history of art, the needs of the urban poor, and Egyptian archaeology: these are lives that are lived in a state of fruitful contradiction. Such contradiction is not, of course, a Jewish monopoly. In the search for harder evidence, let us consider patterns of association. Rahel Varnhagen, born in 1771, was celebrated by members of her coterie with scarcely a mention of her ethnicity; and virtually none of her regular visitors was a Jew. James Simon, born in 1851, did fraternize with some of the elite among his co-religionists, but he also fraternized with the Kaiser, as well as with many lesser gentiles (e.g., museum directors, archaeologists); and his charitable undertakings were spread ecumenically across the city.

Walter Benjamin, born in 1892, inhabits a milieu that is by comparison staggeringly ethnocentric. His close friends from grade school (Ernst Schoen, Alfred Steinfeldt, Willy Wolfradt) were Jews, as were most of his other lifelong friends (e.g., Gershom Scholem, Ernst Bloch). He was mentored by Jews (Ernst Cassirer, Hermann Cohen, Ernst Lewy). His scholarly fellow-travelers (Georg Simmel, Siegfried Kracauer) were Jews. He worked on a translation of Proust (half-Jew) with Franz Hessel (all Jew, though parents converted). When he looked beyond Berlin for intellectual sustenance, he found the Aby Warburg circle in Hamburg, or Theodor Adorno and Max Horkheimer in Frankfurt, or Kafka and Werfel in Prague. He married Jewish (though, in time-honored tradition, he had relationships outside the faith, or, as he phrased it to one Jewish female friend, "Chic goyim are currently my cup of tea"). When he developed complex, not to say neurotic, relations with predecessor texts (Heine, Freud, Buber), they were often Jewish. On one of the many occasions when he quit his parents' house, he moved to the modernist Berlin home of a Jewish friend (Erich Gutkind) that had been designed by a Jewish architect (Bruno Taut). There emerges, in other words, a kind of undertow to what we might imagine as the process of emancipation and assimilation: judging from this example—and Benjamin's case is far from unique—elite Berlin Jews cleave to their own kind just when they are enjoying more acceptance from the general population. It points to the profoundest paradox (again, with the paradox!) of the world into which Benjamin was born. We hear again and again from those who were fortunate enough to survive the horrors that their shock was owing to the fact that they believed themselves to be Germans, just like their Christian neighbors; they were, in the hopeful phrase of the emancipatory period, German citizens of the Mosaic faith. Yet when we reflect on this illusion, we must remember not only the genocide that came afterward but also the society that preceded it, in which most Jews married other Jews, in which *everybody* knew who was and who wasn't a Jew, even when their surnames were indistinguishable, and, to get back to Benjamin, in which high culture Jews tended to hang out with other high culture Jews.

And so, to the question we have asked twice before—what kind of Jew?—we have one answer here that is quite different: the kind whose life is circumscribed by other Jews. Not that this doesn't come with its own contradictions. The boldface names in the Benjamin circle may have been largely Jewish, but—as with Rahel and Simon—this ought not to suggest anything like conventional religious observance. Benjamin grew up in a house where a Christmas tree and an Easter egg hunt were de rigueur; and, as for the barrage of Jewish holidays, there is little reference to them. (We'll hear about an exception.) Benjamin was in fact strongly attracted to the imagery of Christian sainthood; and Gershom Scholem, hardly a disinterested observer, recollected that an earnest discussion of historical process took place in Benjamin's study in front of a print of Grünewald's *Isenheim Altarpiece*, a notably ecstatic and quite unecumenical presentation of Christian suffering. (Scholem also records his argument with Walter about the propriety of the Christmas tree in a Jewish household.) Yet Benjamin was contemptuous of Jews who got baptized, and Scholem reports a scene among Parisian leftists in which Benjamin expressed strong opposition to mixed marriages, an attitude that came as quite a surprise within that multicultural milieu.

Admittedly, this is all par for a certain course that has been played by assimilated Jews in the West for a long time. We know the words to *Silent Night* and *O Come, All Ye Faithful*, we *kvell* over Milton and Bach and Fra Angelico—I, for one, think the *Isenheim Altarpiece* is the greatest painting of all time, even if the temptations of St. Anthony don't look very tempting to *me*—but we also react somewhere on the scale between mockery and alarm when fellow Jews actually try to reformulate themselves as Christians. (I speak from personal experience.)

Benjamin is different because he was given to relentless cultural introspection, much of it focused on what it meant to be a Jew. At a very young age, and with interlocutors far more Jew-identified than he, he professes ignorance: "All I knew [until recently] about Judaism was anti-Semitism and an indeterminate sort of piety. As a religion, it was remote to me, as a nation unknown." At other times, he offers some quite conventional (even embarrassing) generalizations: "The Jews represent an elite in the ranks of intellectuals"; "Jewishness is . . . the noble bearer and representative of the intellect." On yet other occasions, more authentic reflections emerge: "I have discovered that everything that is loftiest in my ideas and in myself as a human being is Jewish. And to put this recognition into a phrase: I am a Jew and if I live as a conscious human being, I live as a conscious Jew."

No surprise that Scholem may be the most eloquent commentator on this subject—indeed, better than Benjamin himself. Describing Benjamin's tendency to alterations and even inconsistency in his thinking, he says, "The word *irgendwie* [somehow, in one way or another] is the stamp of a point of view in the making. I have never heard anyone use this word more frequently than Benjamin," to which he adds in his diary, "one thing he has already settled is that he is no longer *irgendwie* a Jew." Which, when you come to think of it, is a fairly *irgendwie* sort of statement in itself.

Perhaps (*pace* Scholem) "Jew" is just something so inevitably *irgendwie*—isn't that the point of this book?—that we're asking too much of Benjamin to nail it down. It may be preferable to talk about a category that offered some clearer definitions, as it did for James Simon as well: Zionism. From our twenty-first-century perspective, including the Holocaust, the founding of the State of Israel, and the never-ending struggles between Jewish Israelis and Palestinians, Zionism looks like Politics; indeed, to many it looks like ground zero of what we mean in the contemporary world by Politics. When Benjamin is beginning to formulate his attitudes on the subject, as early as 1912, and indeed throughout his lifetime, it also meant Culture.

Once again, Gershom Scholem, himself by origin a Berlin Jew, is the key. The conversations of these two intimate friends from the time of World War I and through the 1920s may have been conducted under the rubric of Zionism; but they were about pacifism, socialism, Marxism, utopianism, and, even more important, about the revival of Judaic learning—both its content and its systems of thought—along with the attempt to integrate that body of wisdom with the education in the German philosophical tradition that brilliant young intellectuals in this time and place had absorbed. Benjamin's contemptuous expression for the alternative to this learned program, such as was being practiced by self-identifying Jews of a less intellectual bent, is "*agricultural Zionism*," a term in which, with hindsight, we can already hear resonances that range from the happy labors of the kibbutz to the displacement of non-Jewish populations in Palestine.

Clearly, history was not on the side of these two brilliant but otherworldly young intellectuals. In 1931, Scholem will say to Benjamin that "Zionism has triumphed itself to death," by which he means that the whole historical and cultural program unearthed, renewed, and promoted by his studies of the Judaic intellectual traditions had been traduced by imperatives that emerged from what is essentially nationalism. That is my term; Scholem puts it more poetically: "Between London and Moscow we strayed into the desert of Araby on our way to Zion, and our own hubris blocked the path that leads to our people."

As it happens, the conflict between these versions of Zionism plays itself out quite literally in Walter Benjamin's life. One could say, rather extravagantly, that his *irgendwie* concerning Zionism was his undoing, considering that it rendered him disastrously unable to commit effectively to the project of emigration, in whatever direction, from Europe. Not that efforts weren't being undertaken. Though the two friends enjoyed several decades of high intellectual conversation, once Scholem established himself in Jerusalem, after 1923, quite a lot of their attention was devoted to a series of projects for enabling Benjamin to make the same trip.

The establishment of humanities studies in Jerusalem shortly after Scholem's arrival gave promise to the project, as did the appointment of a quite open-minded chancellor of the Hebrew University. All that was needed to secure Benjamin's position there was for him to commit to either short- or long-term expatriation, and to learning Hebrew. What follows over the succeeding decade is a mix of tragicomedy, pathos, and psychological enigma. Benjamin recognizes from the start that he is being offered a real professional opportunity that is denied to him at home. He promotes himself for the job, some enthusiastic letters of recommendation are procured, he is accepted, and the chancellor delivers a generous stipend for the purpose of language study, to be paid in advance of Benjamin's arrival in Jerusalem; and in due course he engages a Hebrew tutor.

Then Benjamin breaks off the language lessons with one excuse after another. As time goes by, with no Hebrew and no removal to Palestine, Benjamin's circumstances deteriorate, so that it's not just that he has no worthy academic position but that he has no money at all; soon he will have no citizenship. In the course of these years, he declares himself on seven separate occasions prepared to take up a position in Jerusalem; every time something intervenes. Whatever his qualifications and whatever his intentions, he spent his final decade living a kind of lie, having accepted money on the claim that he would become a reader, indeed speaker, of Hebrew and a professionally Judaic literary scholar, while being either cynically unwilling or helplessly unable to fulfill his obligation. Scholem could leave Berlin behind at age 26, Benjamin not so readily. And the fact that eventually it was not only his financial security but also his life that was at stake only serves to add to the pathos. Declaring himself to be an officially designated Judaic expert played itself out as a bad bargain for Benjamin.

Yet from another perspective, Benjamin would not have been a bad bargain for the Hebrew University, with or without the Hebrew. In fact, his scholarly work, with all its range, variety, and even self-contradiction, bears the consistent imprint of Judaic intellectual traditions. His sense of language as an instrument of complexity and mystery rather than a mere delivery system of signification resembles ancient hermeneutics, with the object transferred from sacred text to literature. His own language—obscure, incantatory, metaphorical—has a decidedly scriptural and Talmudic ring. His model for scholarly learning, or *Lehre*, would not be unfamiliar to the Yeshiva boy that he never was. His dialectical view of the relation between present and past owes something to traditions of biblical interpretation (and not only Jewish ones, to be sure), while issues that are central to the Hebrew bible, like justice, law, and the fear of God, are themselves never very far from his concerns. And his oeuvre over the decades of his writing life moves more or less steadily from work that stands on its own to work that is in the form of commentary, with the same combination of humility and creative intervention that is to be found in the Jewish biblical tradition. No surprise that Scholem, reading Benjamin's essay on Goethe's *Elective Affinities*—the same novel that so inspired Rahel—should say to him, "You ought to become the new Rashi," anointing him by reference to the iconic eleventh-century Talmudic exegete.

Goethe doesn't fit the bill, but some of the most significant literature that Benjamin studied was itself Torah-steeped. Perhaps the most profound literary encounter of all for Benjamin, which never took place in person (though it could have), was with Kafka. There is clearly an element of self-identification—Benjamin notes that Kafka is part mystic and part (as he puts it) "modern big-city dweller." What may tie them even more profoundly with each other and with the Jewish tradition appears at the heart of both *The Trial* and *The Castle*, that is, the imminence of a messiah who does not appear and does not deliver his people. As Scholem said in a letter to Benjamin, "go explain *that* to the goyim."

"Go explain that to the goyim" is in fact a plausible motto for quite a bit of Benjamin's literary and cultural work, but it creates its own sort of frictions within his oeuvre and within his friendship circle. All of these qualities of mind that place Benjamin in my special Jewish pantheon with Rahel Varnhagen and James Simon are at radical odds with the kind of doctrinaire Marxism that Benjamin imbibed, most particularly, from two of his closest companions in his later years: Bertolt Brecht, whom, unlike Kafka, he did meet and indeed associate with extensively, and Asja Lacis, his long-term on-again-off-again lover, who was militantly associated with the Soviet cause until, inevitably, she was sent off to a Kazakhstan gulag by Stalin.

Benjamin did, of course, have Jewish Marxist friends as well; but these two goyim (I use the term as *hommage* to Scholem's vernacular) signal a kind of rejection of ambiguity, of undecidability, of the *irgendwie* that Scholem found so common in Benjamin's discourse. And Benjamin, with the greatest will in the world to be a Marxist, will struggle with his own nature in this regard. As witness some thoughts in one of those unfinished attempts at a magnum opus, his theses on history:

> The class struggle, which always remains in view for a historian schooled in Marx, is a struggle for the rough and material things, without which there is nothing fine and spiritual. Nevertheless these latter are present in the class struggle as something other than mere booty, which falls to the victor. They are present as confidence, as courage, as humor, as cunning, as steadfastness in this struggle, and they reach far back into the mists of time.

That distinction between "rough and material things," on the one hand, and confidence, courage, humor, cunning, etc., on the other, is also a struggle around worldviews, around different Marxisms, or even non-Marxisms, and it is of a piece with all the paradoxes and ambiguities in the life and mind of Benjamin-the-Jew.

I want, though, to withdraw from Karl Marx and the Torah, from Scholem vs. Brecht, from Zionism and the question (once posed to me quite innocently by a gentile Italian who, to my sorrow, was more interested in my mind than my body), "Why is it that Jews are smarter than everybody else?", and turn instead to what I feel is Benjamin's most consistent source of inspiration and the place where he identifies, whether he knew it or not, most fully as a Jew. That place is the City.

There is no great surprise in the association of either Jews or Benjamin with the City. Not that Judaism as a religion or as a social collective was intrinsically urban; quite the contrary, whether in biblical times or in the milieu of the Eastern European shtetl, to which so much in Jewish culture of our present moment can be traced. But the handling of money, the restrictions on land-owning, the narrow range of permissible trades and professions, not to mention the forcible creation of enclaves that could be policed better in towns than in the countryside: all these factors have created both a reality and a perception that Jews are fundamentally city folk. Among Italians, in fact, if you have a city for a surname—Ancona, Milano, Bassano—you're probably a Jew.

So far as Benjamin is concerned, the establishment of his urban credentials need look no further than the concept of the *flâneur*. Whole volumes have been devoted to defining and elaborating the term; let it be sufficient to say that the nineteenth-century city gave rise to the notion that one could be a connoisseur of the streets, strolling attentively in the urban landscape while maintaining a sophisticated detachment. The *flâneur* is at the same time a well-schooled habitué and, by virtue of the profession of observation itself, an outsider who is capable of bringing cosmopolitan analytics to urban phenomena that less acute inhabitants either gape at in uninformed wonder or else ignore. The city in question is generally Paris, whose mid-nineteenth-century demolition and redesign, though motivated originally by health concerns, had turned the urban space into something of a self-proclaiming theater. The poet of these phenomena was Baudelaire, who both theorized the phenomenon of the *flâneur* and versified the world as seen through the eyes of the *flâneur*. But Baudelaire's concept might have nothing like its widespread familiarity in modern thought had Benjamin not become its promoter. He perceived—and it is one of his most brilliant insights—the extent to which the whole phenomenon defined modernity: its capitalist arrangements, its alienation, and its relationship to a newly decentered aesthetics.

Benjamin's grand monument to this set of conceptions, one of his two spectacularly fragmentary candidates for magnum opus, is several hundred pages of essays, vignettes, and quotations circling around the history, geography, architecture, and culture of Paris and finding some sort of fugitive center in the city's early nineteenth-century covered passageways that, in Benjamin's view, sheltered a particular kind of urban experience. The manuscript survived the war by a stroke of luck, received careful editing, and got published as *Passagenwerk* in German and as *Arcades* in English. There is no simple way to describe it, or to determine where to place it on a scale between hoard-of-random-notes and masterpiece-of-collage. It is surrealist, Freudian, and Marxist—all of the above and none of the above—at the same time. And perhaps the best way to sum it up, at least for our purposes, is to say that its combination of attentiveness to the surfaces of the city, on the one hand, and its highly personal free associations off of those surfaces, on the other, define for all time the literary artist as *flâneur* and the modern city as its quintessential site.

With Benjamin as prophet, does that mean that every *flâneur* is a kind of Jew? Or every Jew a kind of *flâneur*? If I guide us to safety from that precipice, it's because Paris is not Berlin, and, above all, because Benjamin was not a *flâneur* in his hometown. If we are to bring him back to Berlin and to the Jews, we have to follow in his footsteps with a different kind of attentiveness on a different urban itinerary.

Benjamin's own words will guide us:

> Losing one's way in a city doesn't mean much. But to lose oneself in a city as one might lose oneself in a forest requires schooling. For that, street names have to speak to the wayfarer like the crackling of dry twigs, and little streets in the city center have to reflect the times of day as clearly as a mountain hollow.

It is a pivotal passage drawn from a piece of autobiographical writing that Benjamin undertook as part of an attempt to rescue himself from an emotional nadir so bleak that he had actually been composing suicide notes. He worked on this essay in urban literature with the hope of exploring a new genre and at the same time producing something more saleable than the rest of what he had been submitting for publication. Ever since I encountered these lines (as well as the book that surrounds them), they have framed my experience as a devotee, and a discoverer, of cities. *Nicht zurechtfinden* as opposed to *sich verirren*: in other words, not having a good enough street map to find your way to San Marco or Rockefeller Center vs. surrendering yourself to a complete immersion in whatever minute accidents the urban landscape hurls into your path. The first option is ignorance (in fact, in an earlier draft of this passage he says it requires nothing but *Unkenntnis*—lack of knowledge). The second option is anything but ignorance: it entails the kind of *schooling* that makes you a sensitive interpreter of urban stimuli with the skills that one ascribes—or at least that city folk ascribe—to the consummate nature guide in the wilderness.

When and where do you get this schooling? In that same earlier draft of the passage, Benjamin is quite explicit about his own case: "Paris taught me this art of straying." The claim is no surprise: he is concurrently reading Proust (some of which he works on translating, along with Franz Hessel, resident of the Bavarian Quarter, whom we quoted back in chapter 2 and who has been his urban walking partner in more than one city), and working on *Arcades*, with its own technique of placing Paris under the microscope. But when he completes the autobiographical manuscript, he removes the reference to Paris. The scene shifts: this book—and I would hazard to say it is his masterpiece and one of the greatest evocations of early life experience that I know—is called *A Berlin Childhood around 1900*. In other words, not Paris, but Berlin, not the musings of an adult urbanite, but the city as seen by a child.

Whatever Paris may have taught Benjamin and however infinitesimal his responsiveness—his *sich verirren*—along the Seine may have been, the place where he chose to enact and to commemorate this sensitivity was the place where he grew up. And the "schooling" that he so exquisitely depicts—the crackling of dry twigs, etc.—comes not "rather late in life" (as he says in an earlier draft of the same materials); rather it gets quite explicitly pinned down circa age eight. If we want to get to know Benjamin and Berlin together, this is the urban itinerary where we must walk in his footsteps.

True to the image of losing oneself in a forest, these footsteps are liable to feel more like wandering in the woods than following an urban grid. Everything about Benjamin's project of recollecting his childhood Berlin sets itself against any sort of objective accuracy; the book is indeed the worst possible travel companion on the streets of the city—unless it's the best. For one thing (and it's the biggest thing), he's not in Berlin when he is writing it. A situation implicit in the book's opening words: "In 1932, when I was abroad, it began to be clear to me that I would soon have to bid a long, perhaps lasting farewell to the city of my birth." From the perspective of later in the decade, when these words were actually composed, it is a masterpiece of understatement, almost of bad faith. He doesn't just *happen* to be out of the country, he is constrained on pain of death into exile. And that casual "perhaps lasting" in regard to this farewell points to the possibility of an unending hell on earth.

So Berlin is going to be present exclusively by memory; and Benjamin will do everything he can to undermine any conventional notion we might have about the retrieval of the past via recollection. Indeed about his reliability as a guide: he has a terrible sense of direction (this we're told in the *Berlin Chronicle*), and it took him thirty years to learn how to read a map, a circumstance that reflects all his real-world ineptitudes, for instance, inability to make himself a cup of coffee, for which his mother bitterly reproached him, thus inducing him to dig in his heels with even more obstinate incompetence and distraction.

What's more, he doesn't *want* to be able to perform these tasks efficiently, nor to present his recollections as though they were perfectly equivalent to the thing itself. "The longing we feel for a place determines it as much as does its outward image." What makes places real to us, in other words, is not their material actuality but our desire for them and the ways that the places invade our dreams via that desire. Underlying it all is a credo evident through much of Benjamin's work, which defines the grandly imaginative texture of these childhood writings: "Memory is not an instrument for exploring the past but its theater." Memory is not, in other words, an apparatus for uncovering the truth, but a mechanism for its fanciful dramatization. (I'm talking to *you*, Sigmund Freud!) Exile, it seems, sentences Benjamin to this theater of memory, since the city can be present only by recollection, that is, through the lens of longing. Thus it must be theatricalized rather than explored; and he embraces this circumstance, just as he embraces his inability to read a map and his refusal—back in the day when these events were *not* filtered through memory—to walk in step with his mother on the streets of Berlin.

Where does that leave him—and us—when it comes to the actual life of the city? If memory is a theater, we might do well to begin with one of the book's early vignettes that stages this matter quite literally. This segment, under the title "Kaiserpanorama" (Figure 5.2), describes the child's fascination with a stereoscopic entertainment that featured some twenty-odd seats around a large wooden structure. Spectators pressed their faces against the double viewfinder and were treated to a sequence of photographs that produced a three-dimensional impact. At set intervals, a bell rang and shortly thereafter a new image hove into view. Everything about this experience enchants young Benjamin: the fact that there was no beginning or end, that there was no accompanying music (which he found "so soporific" in the cinema), that it gave him time to throw himself into the technologically enhanced scene but also, with a certain huffing and puffing, that the scene gave way to another scene. Above all, he loved the opportunity to project himself into exotic far-off places; these were, in fact, the lure of the whole contraption and were advertised on the outside of the building where the Kaiserpanorama was housed.

Coming early in *Berlin Childhood*, this episode models the work itself in miniature, with its thirty-odd brief chapters, each of which focuses on a particular Berlin place or experience. But the relations are full of irony: Benjamin's own literary 3-D pictures do indeed jerk by us one after another, but, whereas in the past he sat in Berlin and gazed at three-dimensional northern fjords and southern palm trees, now, as he writes this book, he is in a foreign place gazing at a zero-dimensional Berlin. The redoubling of here-and-there/now-and-then amounts to an almost infinite regress. The one place he specifically mentions among the scenes in the Panorama is Aix-en-Provence, which he viewed in the stereoscope with rapt attention. Not only is he writing this book from his French exile, but, he tells us, even as a child "the longing such worlds aroused spoke more to the home than to anything unknown." So much so that he tries to believe he once actually played on the sidewalks of the Cours Mirabeau, Aix's grand main boulevard. (Uncanny personal irony: I *did*, not as a child but as a teenager, frequent the Cours Mirabeau; it was a chance meeting on that gracious thoroughfare that brought me my first love. But that's *my* Panorama, not Benjamin's.) Berlin, Aix, Norway, Tahiti: where is home and what counts as being away from home? The overriding issue is longing, and the mechanism of the Kaiserpanorama, as well as of *Berlin Childhood*, produces, in Benjamin's formulation, "the ache of departure," which, given his heavily traveled life, was doubtless inevitable, no matter what the origin and the destination of his many cross-continental movements.

Can you bear one more irony? If you come to Berlin, now in the twenty-first century, you can yourself pull up a seat at the Kaiserpanorama, beautifully preserved in the Märkisches Museum. The rickety wooden chairs, the large polygonal structure, the bell, the thunk of the shifting three-dimensional pictures—all is exactly as Benjamin described. The images, however, are not of far-off places, but of Berlin and its surroundings (the Märkisches Museum, in fact, specializes in the arts and culture of the capital), often in precisely the imperial period when Benjamin was a child, though recently, when they consisted of images from November of 1989, it became evident to me that another iconic chapter of Berlin's history was now being canonized in 3D.

Of course, time travel is at least as exotic as space travel, and in the end pretty much the same thing. If this present book had one of its origins in my visit to the Schönhauser Allee cemetery, where it was possible to view a glorious culture at a high point of its self-expression, the other was sitting at the Kaiserpanorama with Benjamin's little volume in my hands. In the pages of *Ber-*

lin Childhood, the exercise of recollecting the past is plotted on a field of loss, but the exercise itself is a kind of therapy for loss. Walking the streets of Berlin today with Benjamin's book in hand, one can reap the benefits of this therapy, and not only in the theater of a creaky mechanism with clanging gears and dim photographs at the Märkisches Museum, but beyond, in the streets where Benjamin walked. What happens, in short, if we *do* follow some of the vignettes in *Berlin Childhood* as though the book were authored not by Benjamin but by Baedeker?

The Market Hall of Benjamin's childhood—it was directly across from the then family home on Magdeburger Platz—is obliterated, but several of these remarkable structures, part of an enormous public health undertaking at the end of the nineteenth century, are not only extant but reborn as food halls. You can't visit Benjamin's Markthalle V, but at Markthalle IX in Kreuzberg and Markthalle X in Moabit, both elegantly preserved, you can choose either to feast amidst eco-versions of 1890s splendor or else to bring locally made delicacies (e.g., sublime smoked salmon, for me an object of ethnic identification and addiction) home. The purveyors are likelier to be Brooklyn-style hipster dudes than Benjamin's "priestesses of a venal Ceres" with a "bubbling, oozing, and welling" under their skirts. On the other hand, the prediction of ruin, common to nearly every one of his vignettes ("All the images had so decayed that none of them spoke to the original concept of buying and selling"), has been pleasantly contradicted by history.

Crooked Street (*Krumme Straße* to the natives) is still crooked, and there is still a raffish miscellany of shops, though perhaps not so full of "excitement and danger" as in 1900. Benjamin seems to have hated the public swimming pool—during its frequent cleanings he "enjoyed a stay of execution" from compulsory attendance—but at least it is still there, beautifully restored in all its *Jugendstil* elegance. Which, once again, gainsays Benjamin's prediction of oblivion: "It was the seat of a jealous goddess who aimed to lay us on her breast and give us to drink out of icy reservoirs, until all memory of us up above had faded." Nice to know that one can don bathing costume in the twenty-first century and test the validity of his mythological anxiety.

The peacocks still inhabit Peacock Island (Figure 5.3) on the far west of the city, locus of Child Walter's "worst defeat." Granted, we may not arrive there with his regal expectations. The family had its summer place in Potsdam, he tells us, which made them neighbors to the Hohenzollern dynasty at Sans Souci and the Neues Palais. As a consequence, he views his experience there in implacably imperial terms. The finding of a peacock feather, which his parents had vainly promised, was to be a highlight in the "history of [his] reign" (had Benjamin been recently reading Freud's essay on narcissism, with its indelible phrase "His Majesty the Baby"?). The vignette concludes, on the other hand, with his satisfaction in learning to ride a bicycle, as a result of which he came to possess the regions surrounding the family vacation spot "as effortlessly as duchies or kingdoms acquired through marriage into the imperial family." There is no bicycle riding on Peacock Island today, but the birds roam as freely and noisily as ever, the seemingly pasteboard *Schloß* is as fantastical and fragile as ever, and you can try your own skill at imperial acquisition by way of feather. The best I've done is a wisp of a thing about the size of a mid-range caterpillar; I use it as a bookmark in my German edition of *Berliner Kindheit*.

The average guidebook of today won't make nearly as much out of the Landwehr Canal (Figure 5.4), perhaps the most unheralded of the city's waterways, as Benjamin does, but it is worth a close and contemplative look. For young Walter, it remained near home through the rapid sequence of moves undertaken by the family in his early childhood. For him, it stands as an ominous boundary line—"the shoreline of adult life . . . cut off from my own existence"—and it speaks most particularly of death. His playmate Luise von Landau, whose name had him spellbound (perhaps for its aristocratic resonance, though the Landaus were actually ennobled Jews), was among his cohort "the first name on which death had fallen," and he locates her as untouchable from her dwelling across the Canal. From his home vantage point, he gazes at a nearby flower bed convinced (quite fantastically, no doubt; the mature Walter of this volume is always reveling in the misprisions of the child) that it is the "cenotaph" of the buried girl.

Today there are no von Landaus and no flowerbeds, but if you walk along the banks now, and manage to shut out the noise of the traffic and to sidestep the occasional piles of detritus down by the water, you can, like Benjamin, watch the water flow through the canal, "as though intimate with all the sorrow in the world." In fact, his memory was a mis-memory, or rather a memory displaced in time. Happily, Luise did not die in childhood; unhappily, that fate met her decades later in Auschwitz. But as you gaze at the water, you will notice that each of the bridges, however modern its construction, includes a decidedly old-fashioned life preserver, designed perhaps to rescue any Ophelias or Luises threatened with early demise.

While in the neighborhood, you may wish to pay *hommage* to two sites of supreme comfort and security for the child Benjamin. Strictly speaking, there is no longer a "Corner of Steglitzer and Genthiner," the title of one of his vignettes and the location of the bay window from which his house-bound aunt, in her murky apartment atop a steep staircase, held court and seemed, like some fairy-tale character, to rule "over whole rows of streets without ever setting foot in them." Steglitzer Straße is now Pohlstraße, and—yet greater indignity inflicted by the passage of time—the two streets no longer quite meet, their conjunction replaced by the loading dock of an unusually ugly furniture warehouse. Yet in a kind of accidental fulfillment of Benjamin's claim that this neighborhood was exceptionally untouched since his early years, there remains, not exactly in the right place and doubtless not exactly in the right style, a finely decorated corner building with something that might pass for a bay window. He declares that, since his childhood, the veil that covered this happy location has fallen away; perhaps we can put a little bit of it back.

More challenging to put the veil back at "Blumeshof 12," another vignette title and another safe haven, in this case provided by his grandmother Schönflies, abetted by his grandmother Benjamin, who lived across the way. There is no Blumeshof in modern Berlin, no "Elysium . . . inhabited by shades of immortal yet departed grandmothers," but if you comb the groundscape, as I have done, you'll find a largely effaced remainder of pavement at the same diagonal that the old maps indicate for this obliterated address. And if you follow it a little ways toward Lützowstraße, you'll enter a tiny bit of parkland with some private allotments where modern citizens have planted a garden of big garish flowers: no Elysium, to be sure, but, at least in the right season, the "Blume" in Blumeshof hasn't quite perished. The vast Tiergarten, on the other hand, forms a quite passable replica of its early twentieth-century condition. If you pursue the route he took from home (though it's no longer a labyrinth, and you'll have to bring your own Ariadne with you), you'll enter the park directly in front of what used to be James Simon's mansion, and you'll approach the same statues, of Queen Luise and Frederick Wilhelm III, that Benjamin enjoyed observing. You can admire the same, or possibly replica, pedestals; but, as you enter the space that transfixed young Walter, be sure to follow the instructions that admonish visitors, "Please close the gate on account of rabbit nuisance."

I wish the loggias, subject of the very first vignette in *Berlin Childhood*, were as plentiful today as they were in Benjamin's time, and as open to our view as they were to his. Berlin is still a city of magnificent courtyards, as you'll find if you prowl around the Hackescher Markt—too dangerously Far East for Walter's protective mother ever to have schlepped him, though a mere stone's throw from the somewhat fictive site of Moses Mendelssohn's resting place. Nevertheless, one can, with a sufficiently sharp eye and some willingness to trespass among possibly private spaces, manage to intrude upon those unspoiled courtyards that still sport rows of sculpted balconies. Even then, though, I can't promise all of Benjamin's resonances. For the intoxicating air that "was still present in the vineyards of Capri where I held my beloved in my arms," Capri itself is probably more promising. Nor can I guarantee such a world of meaning—"it is precisely this air that sustains the images and allegories which preside over my thinking"; "everything in the courtyard became a sign or hint to me"—as he found there. On the other hand, during those long, *long* Berlin summer evenings (in late June it can be quite possible to read a book outside at 10:00 PM), if you come upon one of these majestic enclosures in Tiergarten or Charlottenburg, you can just about believe his claim that in this setting "space and time come into their own and find each other."

Which explains precisely why Benjamin placed this as his first chapter: the memory of the loggias is an attempt at therapy for all his life's dislocations in space and time. Solace, he says, "lies in their uninhabitability for one who himself no longer has a proper abode." It's worth recollecting that he tells us he has written the whole book as a kind of inoculation: the proper tincture of the disease can fight the disease. A little longing for the loggia will be good medicine.

Loggias are only the tip of an iceberg. The most radical and therefore riskiest inoculation performed by these writings is the relentless emphasis upon the extraordinary level of privilege that this child enjoys, all of it now lost. Indeed, if we are searching for the record of what it meant to be a wealthy, bourgeois Berlin Jew in the heyday of that possibility, with, mutatis mutandis, the same kinds of self-assurance evident in the monuments of Schönhauser Allee or in James Simon's visit to the Fasanenstraße synagogue with Kaiser Wilhelm in tow, these are the pages in which to find it. And the fact that we are here seeing it through the eyes of a child only serves to make this vision the more acute, the inoculation more difficult to distinguish from the disease.

If you are accustomed to the pose of slight discomfiture with which middle-class persons nowadays allude to their affluence, it comes as something of a surprise, almost a social embarrassment, to hear, "my parents being wealthy, we moved every year . . . to summer residences not far from home." That comes from the *Berlin Chronicle*, with its characteristically direct utterances on the subject, but the later, more carefully curated work is a veritable bank vault of rich people's stuff: jewels, linens, china, networks of retail suppliers (themselves clearly of lower social standing, such that Emil Benjamin could yell at them on the telephone), glass-fronted but locked cabinets filled with tempting but inaccessible luxuries. Young Walter mythologizes the family's extensive collection of Onion Pattern Meissen, and he recollects vividly his mother's special occasion jewel "with a sparkling yellow gem encircled by some even larger stones of various colors—green, blue, yellow, pink, purple." These are a few of his favorite things.

With *things* come people. The servants who called his mother *Gnädige Frau*, which he misunderstood as *"Näh-Frau"* or "Madam Needlework"; the nursemaid who awakened the slug-a-bed child with a freshly baked apple; the laundress whose meticulous practice enabled him later to "draw truth from literature" in just the way he had operated from inside and outside in releasing the "dowry" of the socks she had so meticulously rolled up. Alternatively, there is the housemaid who, by accident or design (it's never made clear), had left a gate open, thus enabling a nighttime burglary of all the house's contents. This is of a piece with a roster of class anxieties as voluminous as the possessions that are being guarded. The child becomes nearly delusional with fear in response to the admonition that he must attach the chain before opening the door a crack at the advent of a visitor. And he obsesses over ambulances, police vans, shuttered hospital windows, and fire alarm boxes, "altars before which supplicants address their prayers to the goddess of misfortune."

Still, there are places of wealth and security that are free from such anxieties. The aunt of "Steglitzer Ecke Genthiner" in her luxurious home allows Walter to play with the model of a complete working mine, which only serves to solidify the difference between little rich boys and coal miners. And when the Schönflies grandmother, also in deluxe surroundings, shows off the postcard collection from her far-flung travels, it proves in his eyes that the whole world is nothing more than a colony of this household.

If you want to know how certain rich Berliners lived in 1900, then, this is the place to look. But even in the twenty-first century, the opulence of Berlin remains accessible. Not, perhaps, the curio cabinets full of Meissen china, but the veritable building stock of the city. If you maintain, as I do, the mental photograph of Berlin in 1945 as a place of total destruction—estimates vary between one-third and three-quarters of the buildings in some state of ruin—then the biggest surprise you will have in coming to Berlin, bigger even than any of the surprises about the continuities of Jewish culture, will be the fact that you can walk through the city for days, whether in swanky Charlottenburg, or radical chic Prenzlauer Berg, or "marginal" Moabit, or sprawling Kreuzberg, no matter which half of the divided city you traverse, including those parts said to have been left unattended by the impoverished DDR regime, and you will see block after block of architectural grandeur (Figure 5.5). Just as young Walter, within his narrower geographical compass, saw it.

Of course, the surprise in Benjamin's memoir is not only the ostentation of wealth, but the ostentation of Jewish wealth. The pages of *Berlin Childhood* play the most devious of all their games with the Jewish question, and that may be their most telling piece of social portraiture. For the most part, it is a game of silence and innuendo on this life-or-death subject. In the earlier draft of his book, Benjamin (speaking of himself in the third person) refers to the West End, "where the class that had pronounced him one of its number resided in a posture compounded of self-satisfaction and resentment that turned the district into something like a ghetto held on lease." It's a sentence worthy of careful appreciation, as social class turns to (implicit) ethnic identity and thence to the ominous sense of possible dislodgment—all without the use of the word *Jew*.

I had a much loved cousin (past tense, alas) who grew up in a part of my family that had emancipated themselves to the extent of—simultaneously—avant-garde life in Greenwich Village and a sprawling permanent residence in Connecticut. Around age eighteen, owing to something that was said to him at his high school, he went to his mother with some alarm, and asked, "Are we Jewish?" I should add that his foreign-born grandfather, whom he saw regularly, was so unassimilated that he never learned to read the Roman alphabet and could usually be seen in an easy chair scanning the *Daily Forward*, his eyes moving unremittingly from right to left. Benjamin's writing about his childhood—and therefore I assume the life itself—is a monument to my cousin Jon, and to this remarkable Jewish phenomenon of absorption, assimilation, oblivion, and denial.

In fact, the exercise of wealth in these pages seems almost relentlessly gentile. Christmas, Benjamin says in the *Berlin Chronicle*, "divided the rich from the poor." And there was no question on which side this family belonged. The great spaces of Grandmother Schönflies's apartment, often shuttered during the rest of the year, came into their own, he tells us, at Christmas. Ritually, the glittering tree was revealed at a magic moment of the holiday celebrations, while the tables nearby groaned under a cargo of decorations, marzipan candy, and children's presents. The tree is presented even more iconically at the Benjamin house itself, procured with great care at the Christmas market and coursing through its life cycle until, with the singing of a carol about the Christ Child ("Alle Jahre wieder / Kommt das Christus Kind / Auf die Erde nieder, / Wo wir Menschen sind"), the tree is revealed in its full glory. It may be recalled that later, when the two friends were already young men, Gerschom Scholem had been scandalized by the Christmas tree in the Benjamins' household. One can only be thankful for Scholem's sake that he wasn't on the premises back in 1900. Nor was Easter much different. The house is once again awash in special finery, and little Walter burrows through it excitedly searching for Easter eggs.

Why is Hanukkah never mentioned at the Benjamin Yuletide? Why is little Walter hunting for Easter eggs rather than the *afikomen*? Why is it that when he details the grandeur of the family silver, the only pieces he cites are lobster forks and oyster forks? *Paradoxie.*

The hidden Jew does come cautiously out of hiding on occasion. Those visits to his widowed aunt Lehmann in her secure perch of an apartment, which, he says, "her good North German name had secured her the right to occupy over the course of a generation," are the occasion of a regularly performed genealogical monologue on her part. Recounting her native region, Mark Brandenburg, she recollected all the villages and all the relatives, whose names "so often proved to be exactly the same." She "knew the relationships by marriage, the various places of residence, the joys and the sorrows of all the Schönfliesses, Rawitschers, Landsbergs, Lindenheims, and Stargards." Now, her sons and grandsons resided, as she did, in the Old West End of Berlin, "in streets that bore the names of Prussian generals and, sometimes also of the little towns [the members of her family] had left behind."

Benjamin is playing a dazzling game of evasion here. The

Schönfliesses, Rawitschers, Landsbergs, etc., despite the epic quality with which they are presented by Tante Lehmann and Benjamin himself, are, of course, all Jews (the *Jüdisches Adress-buch für Groß-Berlin* lists 46 Landsbergs, along with 54 Lands-bergers, and one can hunt profitably for several of these families in Schönhauser Allee), but that goes unmentioned. And his aunt's "good North German name," despite the fact that there are almost 100 Lehmanns in the *Jüdisches Adressbuch*, seems to possess landed rights of residence very much in the style of the nobility, as witness her privileged abode in Berlin. The fact that towns and surnames were identical could lead in either direction, signifying, alternatively, ancient noble fiefdoms or else Jews who had been summarily identified by their place of residence. But the whole thing tips toward the aristocratic by the introduction of those Prussian generals—you can't get more goyish than that—whose names seem to have spanned both the Mark Brandenburg and Berlin's Old West End. Which is just, in their own way, what the Schönfliesses et al. have managed to do.

I called this a game, but there is really no way of knowing whether Benjamin is playing with the reader or whether his own thinking about these subjects—especially when he is thinking through the child—is somehow involuntarily stuck between identities. Perhaps it doesn't matter. But one vignette in *Berlin Childhood*, placed, perhaps significantly, last in some versions of his compilation, addresses this matter more directly, or at least less *in*directly; and, in this case, the voice of the adult shadows more closely the voice of the child.

The various forms of the word *Jew* appear so infrequently in Benjamin's book as to seem almost a deliberate suppression. In "Two Enigmas," he descants upon the consonants in the name of his teacher, Fräulein Pufahl, noting that if it didn't have vowels, it would be "like some Semitic text" (he thus avoids the *J* word); therefore, he declares, by what logic one isn't sure, it would cease to be mere calligraphy and become "the root of all virtues." He names the Chosen People more directly in "Misfortunes and Crimes" (coincidence? probably not) by reference to the Angel of Death—his subject is the ominously shuttered windows of St. Elizabeth's Hospital—but he does so, it seems, only by way of comparison to himself, as though he and the Jews were quite separate entities.

But then we have the episode suggestively entitled "Erwachen des Sexus." By comparison to everything that precedes it, this brief vignette is veritably awash in Judaism. It is the season of the Jewish New Year, we are told, and a relative has been deputed to lead the boy into the Reform Synagogue for services. But all is not as suitably observant as it seems. Walter's parents obviously want no part of this transaction, the relative in question is a "virtual stranger," to whom the boy has an aversion, and the choice of the Reform synagogue—our narrator isn't even sure of this, as he recalls the episode—is merely based on the fact that his mother "felt some sympathy on account of family tradition." Plus, for his own part, the boy harbors a "suspicion of religious ceremonies, which promised only embarrassment."

So far as a commitment to being a Jew—a religious, synagogue-haunting Jew, at any rate—it couldn't get any worse. Except it does. Young Walter gets lost on the way to the appointment, the clock keeps ticking, and he realizes that he can't enter the synagogue on his own (even if he could find it), since he hasn't got the tickets. (Another little dig, I can only assume: the house of God shouldn't require tickets, but it does.) He never gets to the shul, never meets the hated distant relative, never gets to hear the shofar being blown.

At the point of realizing this, two emotions crowd in upon him. First, desperation that he'll never make the appointed meeting, and second a "wave . . . of utter indifference." At that moment, awash in Berlin on his own and without a realizable destination, sacred or otherwise, the boy experiences

a dawning sensation of pleasure, wherein the profanation of the holy day combined with the pandering of the street, which here, for the first time, gave me an inkling of the services it was prepared to render to awakened instincts.

End of the vignette and, in some versions, the end of the book. The whole episode, titled and framed by the onset of puberty, is an electrifying piece of blasphemy. There are many indications in *Berlin Childhood* that this boy, when he grows up, will be a hunter after sexual satisfaction, that he will leave his mother's care for that of the streets, where "not the cleanest of hands" will minister to him, that the Ariadne to be found in the middle of his adult labyrinth will not be someone like the childhood crush who lurked at the center of the Tiergarten maze, but rather a prostitute. Yet what is thrilling in this explicit and climactic episode is that the echt Jew in Benjamin, who has been kept so rigorously offstage, should make his entrance as the reject cast aside in favor of the sex hunter.

Not that the two are completely incommensurable. Though the book's title refers to 1900, which pegs Benjamin at eight years old, the probable age of the child referred to in the vignettes varies widely. At this moment, late in the book, he has clearly reached something like the canonical thirteen. The bar mitzvah is said to signal the attainment of manhood; Benjamin, however, has opted for an alternative ceremony to that end. It is, of course, a different *kind* of ceremony. The synagogue fixes authority and identity in one spot. But young Benjamin cannot find his way there. In fact, to describe those futile attempts at locating the relative and the house of worship, he uses that same verb—*sich nicht zurecht finden*—that represented for him mere ignorance as regards the urban landscape. The hunt for sexual satisfaction in the streets will turn out to be precisely that *schooling*—developing the ability to recognize the dry twigs, the mountain hollow, and so forth—which enables the young man to become a consummate reader of the city.

So I ask our ritual question: what kind of Jew was Walter Benjamin? A very bad Jew, some would say. Rahel Varnhagen said she hated being "ein Schlemihl und eine Jüdin," and James Simon was castigated for being too much of a German and not enough of a Palestine-conscious Zionist. Then there's Benjamin, with his Easter Egg hunts and his family treasure of oyster forks, who blew off Rosh Hashanah in preference to a career of getting laid. The sum total, what these lives contained and what they didn't contain, is bound to drive us into a banal recitation about "culture." Somehow, the Torah and the cheder, the wanderings in the desert and the intricacies of rabbinical hermeneutics, the relentless patriarchy and the proverbial mother, even the prejudices and the pogroms—in short, those things that we think of as inextricable from the identity, the theology, the history of the Jew—continue to leave a space, or rather continue to *forge* a space, in which alternatives, even violently contrasting alternatives, flourish.

Quite often, whether explicitly or implicitly, that space is the denial of being a Jew or the refusal to be the Jew of the synagogue or of Zionism, leaving such replacements as wholly secular forms of love, friendship, and conversation, or else a credo of aesthetics with ambitions to proselytize it among the masses, or else an intellectual project that both embodies and defies the millennial Hebraic traditions, which are common even among those members of this troubled, and trouble-making, minority who profess ignorance or implacable opposition (I'm talking about *you*, Karl Marx!). I lined up those alternatives as *hommage*, respectively, to my three Berlin Jews; in fact, though, Walter Benjamin, with his circles of rich and troubled friendship, his tales for children and radio audiences, and his combination of absorption and rejection as regards The Book (as in "The People of the Book"), manages to embrace them all. The map of this variegated life can still be drawn upon the streets of Berlin.

Epilogue: **Recollections, Reconstructions**

The paradox at the heart of this book (again, with the paradox!) is the claim that Berlin feels so Jewish even with most of its Jews gone. For me, the living presence of the city's Jewish culture is an article of faith, just as the living presence of Virgil and Hadrian and Michelangelo is an article of faith when I stroll through Rome: it's partly monuments, partly memories, and mostly the belief that the present is determined, even overdetermined, by the past. Rome is indeed the appropriate object of comparison for Berlin, and not just because of its importance in my own life. Both cities are filled with ruins and recollections. In one case, the rises and falls can be measured in millennia, in the other case little more than a century; but in both instances we are left with a metropolis where history confronts us, slaps us in the face, at every step. (Thanks, I needed that.) It's also true that in Berlin, just as in Rome, history *is* ruin, and the note of absence will always sound louder than that of presence. Does the knowledge of a Jewess's salon in 1825 or a Jewish plutocrat's art mania in 1904 or a band of brilliant young Jewish intellectuals in 1920 bring the stones of the city to life, post-1945, post-1989, and post-whatever other radical changes contemporary life has brought everyone? Does all this make today's Berlin more Jewish?

All I can say is, go there and see. You'll have no trouble finding markers, since the Federal Republic of Germany, in Berlin more than anywhere else, has made it policy that the horrors of the past, as well as the cultural contributions made by the murdered subset of its former population, never be forgotten. Whether these sorts of commemorations testify more to the life or the death of Berlin's golden age is open to question, however. One scarcely finds much satisfaction, for instance, in Walter-Benjamin Platz (Figure 6.1), a former parking lot bearing no geographical relation to any of the writer's many residences in the city and now transformed into a pompous Italianate piazza ringed with high-priced apartments and shops. If that act of memorialization seems a little bloated in comparison to the bohemian existence of its eponym, quite the opposite can be said of Rahel-Varnhagen-Promenade (Figure 6.2), a pedestrian (in more than one sense) thoroughfare that commemorates the elegant doyenne by means of a notably drab bit of Kreuzberg hardscrabble, again identifiable with no real estate in Berlin where she actually operated. A shade more realness is to be found in Mitte's Gartenstraße, at the James Simon Public Baths: not only is it a beautifully repaired structure in the New Objectivity style, built in 1880 but still in active use by the swimmers of Berlin, it also has a genuine connection with the name that it sports, since he paid for it. Still, public baths are not perhaps the essence for which we most remember James Simon.

On the other hand, thinking of that ubiquitous ancient inscription, SISTE VIATOR—stay voyager—I would say it is definitely worth our time to stop and gaze at some of the plaques that commemorate the dwelling places of Berlin's past citizens. Walter Benjamin is a bit of a problem in this regard since he resided in at least seven Berlin locations (not to mention dossing down with countless equally impecunious friends). The city apparently decided to narrow it down to his one real adult residence at Prinzregentenstraße 66, where, if you bend your body across a locked fence and gaze at the side of the building, you can read a brief text that gives equal time to his life and his death (as I, obviously, do not). James Simon fares much better, even leaving aside the public baths. Besides the recognition in the Neues Museum and the future James Simon Gallery on Museum Island, two of his residences, at Bundesallee 23 and in Tiergartenstraße, attest to his civic importance, the latter providing an eloquent brief bio that concludes with the stirring words, "He represents a public spiritedness that in 1933 was violently destroyed."

My favorite plaque, though, belongs to Rahel, located on the site of her earliest salon, at Jägerstraße 54–55 (see Figure 3.2). In elegantly etched relief lettering that surrounds a silhouette-style likeness, vaguely in period for Rahel, one can read a brilliantly concise verbal portrait (with apologies for much lost in translation): "Here [in her salon] men and women undertook swordplay with words, practiced criticism with spirit and wit, wrestled with truth." This is followed by an even more untranslatable quotation from Rahel herself, hinging upon the multiple meanings, legal and philosophical, of *Eigentum*: "Personal property? All we own is that within us which no one can imitate. That is our very essence."

You may, on the other hand, be thinking of a different kind of marker—death rather than life—of a sort in which Berlin abounds. The determination never to forget expresses itself all over the city in public installations, large and small, dedicated not to a single Varnhagen or a Simon or a Benjamin but to vast numbers of horrifically victimized citizens. Anyone who views these undertakings, or the impulses motivating them, with unmixed feelings, positive or negative, possesses a single-mindedness that is foreign to me. To be sure, it is vital and life-affirming that the twenty-first century build monuments so that the present and the future not let this chapter of the past sink into oblivion. On the other hand, holocaust memorialization sometimes seems like an industrial juggernaut, complete with public relations, profit-and-loss statements, and all the tendencies of mass communication to blanket the world with its own slick messages. Whoever first said "There's no business like shoah business" said a mouthful.

When I approach these memorial shrines—I like the German term *Mahnmal* because it contains both the idea of monument and the idea of warning—the first thing I feel (though I scarcely admit it, even to myself) is a buoyancy of spirit, a gut reaction embodying a certain joyous gratitude; I bask in the belief that they remember, they regret, they care. But this is followed by a rush of negatives. First, comes the knee-jerk cynicism, as I find myself in front of yet another money maker in the holocaust industry designed to appeal to busloads of teary-eyed foreign tourists making some kind of compensatory anti-aliyah. I graduate from this rather sophomoric response to some more serious questions. Does the monument in front of me serve to awaken a consciousness of man's inhumanity to man or rather to trivialize and package it? Is it life-affirming or death-affirming?

Next—and most self-critically of all—I ask myself whether the distance I am placing between myself and these enterprises is the product of my own cowardice, my inability to face *any* terrors (I never, but *never*, see horror movies: why should I pay to have nightmares after witnessing *Friday the 13th* or *Cannibal Apocalypse*? Frankly, I have a little trouble with *Sweeney Todd* and *Don Giovanni*), but in particular those that, ever so indirectly, touch on me. The truth of the matter is that I cannot bear to think about any particulars of the six million, that I have never been to Dachau or Theresienstadt, and that this book is written as a kind of therapy, or something like Plato's *pharmakon*, which was both poison and cure. Finally, though, I come to an acceptance of the widely agreed upon fact that there is no remedy for the horror, neither in grand monumentalization nor in the consciousness of a single observer.

In all this, as it plays itself out in Berlin, I find one small place of affirmation. Walter Benjamin's friend Theodor Adorno famously asked whether there could be poetry after Auschwitz; the same question might be asked about painting, music, and the task of memorialization itself. My answer (his, too, in effect) is a cautious *yes, maybe.* The task of commemoration, all the more so because it is so ubiquitously practiced in Berlin and because the goal of rising to the heights/depths of its subject matter is so unattainable, raises the bar for the artistic and the historical imagination. If you're going to be viewing these monuments as (you should pardon the expression) a holocaust tourist in Berlin, it is that exercise of the imagination that you should be looking for. What do these monuments manage to evoke, where do they leave us?

And it is with that in mind that I approach this crowded field. The competing star attractions—I think of them as the Renata Tebaldi and Maria Callas of my early days as an opera groupie—are the Jewish Museum and the Holocaust Memorial, each the product of a celebrity Jewish-American architect. Daniel Libeskind's museum advertises itself as three thousand square meters of space covering two thousand years of German-Jewish history. Peter Eisenman's monument—officially, the Memorial to the Murdered Jews of Europe—also brandishes impressive numbers: 2,711 concrete slabs arrayed over five acres of choice real estate near the Brandenburg Gate. Both have been objects of a great deal of attention, quite a bit of it (especially in the case of the Museum) critical. Both deserve the close and careful attention of anyone interested enough to have got this far in the present volume.

By the standards of my question—what do these monuments evoke?—the Jewish Museum deserves some credit for focusing on many centuries of history and not just on the twelve nightmare years, though predictably the rooms illustrating 1933–1945 are always the most crowded with sightseers. The problem with the place, besides the fact that the actual materials exhibited are a bit thin and often consist of replicas, is that the building insists on telling you what to think. The axis of continuity, the axis of exile, the axis of the holocaust; the garden of exile; the "voids" (I can't help thinking of the joke about the Jewish immigrant who is asked to spell "avoid" and responds "vot void?"): every space is allegorical, and nothing is allowed to speak for itself. And the materials on display, though occasionally surprising, informative, or poignant—check out the family albums from some of the Schönhauser Allee families, along with the vending machine containing kosher gummi bears—can hardly make their presence felt.

The Holocaust Memorial is quite the opposite. The monument as we see it above ground is uncompromisingly abstract. While inviting some comparison to a graveyard (the older, less adorned segments of Schönhauser Allee spring to mind), these cold blank forms insist on their status as tabulae rasae inviting individual contemplation but specifying nothing. And the patterns of the pathways, bringing visitors down to the depths where they risk losing their bearings only to deliver them again into the streets of Berlin, produce in me, at least, an uncanny ambiguity of sensations between regimentation and fear, quite appropriate to the history they are recalling. Among these grey blocks, I have seen mini-clad sunbathers and children playing hide-and-seek, I have seen visitors variously perplexed, contemptuous, impassive, and grieving. And I respect them all. This monument does its work by an equivocal answer to Adorno's question. Yes, there can be monuments after Auschwitz, but only if they renounce every form of representation: no names, no pictures, nothing but low-luster screens on which to project the (literally) unimaginable.

The truth is that if you're a reader of this book and you go to Berlin, you are bound to visit these two urban attractions, and you don't need me to tell you what to think about them. I urge you, however, to leave some openings in your terror itinerary for less prominent memorials. For me at least, the Jewish Museum talks too much, leaving me little room for my own thoughts. The Holocaust Memorial, on the other hand, though I continue to find it memorable and uplifting, may err in the other direction: when the tabula is so totally rasa, it leaves my mind a little *too* free. Does it, in short, fail to offer me the material out of which I can practice my own evocations?

I'm not sure I would have formulated this need were it not for several Berlin projects, quieter and less publicized than the work of Libeskind and Eisenman, that strike the right balance between what they tell me and what I am permitted to feel. First of all, the *Stolpersteine*. As you walk through the streets of Berlin, look down at the pavement. When you notice—and you *will* notice, since there are many thousands of them—a shiny little brass block about four inches square hammered into the sidewalk, stop. You may even stumble: *Stolpersteine*, in fact, means "stumbling stones." The plaque won't overwhelm you with information, just HERE LIVED, followed by a name and a birth year, then DEPORTED, with a date and destination—AUSCHWITZ, MAIDANEK, SACHSEN-HAUSEN, or one of those other terrible names—then MURDERED, and a date. Occasionally, there are some variations in the formula that precedes the death date: SUICIDE or MEDICAL HELP DENIED or DEPRIVED OF RIGHTS, HUMILIATED, FLED TO HIS DEATH. And very occasionally, something like SURVIVED ARGENTINA or FLED PALESTINE. Once you have read the inscription, look up. You are standing in front of a building, or the successor to a destroyed building, from which those persons were forcibly extracted.

One summer we actually lived in such a building, rebuilt after the war but fundamentally in its early twentieth-century shape. The persons memorialized—and there is an extensive biograph-ical network available on the *Stolperstein* website, so you can research them all—were the quite ordinary owners of a little furniture store that was itself in the building. I can't say that the stumbling stones summoned Niche and Simon Scherl back from death and obscurity, but they did their work nonetheless (Figure 6.3). The stones were incredibly shiny (in fact, the project includes a little army of volunteer polishers), and no matter how dulling my routine of entering and leaving the house might have been—and I crossed the threshold quite a lot, since I was combing the city as research for this book—the brilliant sparkle of the two Scherl memorializations cut through the fog. There was something brilliant about the way they glistened more than anything else on the street, and it was a street with a lot of fairly cheap glitter. Perhaps full-time Berliners learn to routinize this experience; I couldn't. But I should add, with apologies if it appears scandalous, that my reaction wasn't one of deep mourning or grand righteousness. Those two little stones seemed to shine a light into my life.

If you're tired of stumbling on stones in the center of Berlin, take the S-Bahn to Grunewald in the leafy suburban west of the city—the neighborhood, eventually, of Walter Benjamin's upwardly mobile parents and many other wealthy Jews. No need to leave the train station, even, just find your way to a disused part of the structure labeled GLEIS 17, or Track 17 (Figure 6.4). If you enter from the train station, rather than the street, you are largely deprived of any explanation for what you are about to see, which is a good thing. You find yourself on a pair of train platforms framing a set of tracks that are out of use; in fact, you can simply climb down across the tracks from one side of the platform to another. But apart from these railway remnants, there seems to be nothing there.

Then you will begin to notice that at the edge of the platform on which you are walking, there are, as it turns out, 186 engraved metal inscriptions commemorating the deportations, day by day, that took place from this train junction. For instance,

14.11.1941 / 956 Juden / Berlin–Minsk
17.11.1941 / 730 Juden / Berlin–Kowno
27.11.1941 / 1035 Juden / Berlin–Riga

Getting the big picture requires that you take a long, slow walk along the two sides of the tracks, calculating the calendar and the numbers of individuals transported. The words "deported" or "murdered" are never used—indeed, there's no verb. Only a date, a quantity, a destination, and the endlessly repeated words *Berlin* and *Juden*. Even the morphology, that is to say, the engraved slash "/" that connects, or doesn't connect, the terms is powerful. The first time I visited Gleis 17, I gave myself a narrative, to determine how many Jews were deported from Berlin on the day that I was born in New York. Was I disappointed that my birthday didn't appear, that the extermination process, like other businesses, sometimes allows itself a three-day weekend?

Having failed in this goal, I continued my walk and paid close attention to the actual information on the 186 metal pieces. For more than half the time span depicted (beginning in October 1941), the majority destination is the nearby Theresienstadt, with occasional deportations to eastern ghettoes like Warsaw and Riga; the numbers to Theresienstadt are always quite small, unlike those to the ghettoes. Then Auschwitz starts to crop up, with much larger numbers. The numbers (numbers of Jews once again) tell their own story, and not just the quantity. There is an appalling frequency of round numbers—100, at first (later 1000), except that occasionally it's 99 or 101, suggesting failure to meet the goal or extra zeal, respectively—all of it reminding us, as does the very presence of the information, that the mass murder was both plotted and documented in a fanatically meticulous way, indeed with industrial production as its goal. It's instructive as well to look at the bell curve of quantities, which begin small, rise to a maximum (2.3.1943 / 1758 Juden / Berlin–Auschwitz) and end up small again as the undertaking proceeds to within a few weeks of the war's end. And, of course, there are those weekends off, plus Christmas, Easter, and all the other holy days on the calendar.

One final entry in the bustling memory industry. A few chapters back we visited the Bavarian Quarter, with its stately residential buildings and its distinguished roster of Jewish and non-Jewish residents during the first decades of the twentieth century. If you walk those streets today and lift your eyes upward, you will see atop the lamp posts mini-street signs with some of the following:

> Excursions by Jewish Youth groups of more than twenty people are forbidden. July 10, 1935
> Jews are expelled from all choral groups. August 16, 1933

Sauntering a few more blocks along, you read:

> Jewish members of the greater German chess association are expelled. July 9, 1933
> Jews may not use the public beach at Wannsee. August 22, 1933

The dates are very specific, and very much in the past, yet little concession is made to the fact that these laws are no longer on the books. In fact, when they first went up, they produced a general frisson of terror: were they part of the problem or part of the (final) solution? ("Art or no art, the boundaries of good taste have been overstepped," declared a city official.) In response to the uproar, miniature addenda in very small print were attached below each sign: "Memorial. Places of Remembrance in the Bavarian Quarter. Ostracism and Disenfranchisement, Expulsion and Murder of Berlin Jews in the Years from 1933 until 1945." Which reassured viewers that Jews nowadays, should there be any interested in so doing, were in fact permitted to swim at Wannsee.

The project consists of some eighty tiny memorials blanketing the neighborhood, each citing a regulation that oppressed Berlin's Jewish citizens. It is the work of Renata Stih and Frieder Schnock, a brilliant married couple of artist/provocateurs (total disclosure: they are friends of mine), who have gone on to even eerier projects, like fitting out Berlin city buses with regular time tables and regular stops, except that they had final destination signs such as BERGEN-BELSEN and TREBLINKA. That project, from 1995, must have emigrated a little too far over the boundaries of civic taste; as a result, it was not put into practice. But here, in their successful entry for a memorial in the Bavarian Quarter, they overturned the whole industry of monumental, single-site commemorations in favor of something inescapable and ubiquitous throughout the neighborhood. Even more radically, instead of the death-of-the-Jews imagery that would characterize the Eisenman memorial, the *Stolpersteine*, or the Grunewald railway track (all of which came later), they made us think about the *life* of the Jews under National Socialism.

Not just the life but, at least at the beginning, the ordinary, the trivial, the quotidian. If you try to follow the chronology of prohibitions, you begin with some minor disturbances, as mentioned above: no choir, no beach, no chess. But as you walk along, you see more. Forbidden to buy newspapers and magazines (February 17, 1942), soap and shaving cream (June 26, 1941), cigarettes and cigars (June 11, 1942). Life's ordinary necessities curtailed: marketing only between 4:00 and 5:00 PM (July 4, 1940), eggs, milk, and meat made unavailable (June 22, 1942, July 10, 1942, September 18, 1942, respectively), warm clothes confiscated (note the season: January, 1942), public transport first limited (March 24, 1942), then excluded altogether (April 24, 1942). Children are not immune: Jews and "Aryans" cannot play together (1938); at first public schools are closed to them (November 15, 1938), then all schools (June 20, 1942); and even when they could go to school, they couldn't use public transportation unless the distance was more than five kilometers (March 24, 1942). On the one hand, petty, cruel, and meaningless gestures: no cakes (February 14, 1942—Valentine's Day!), no pets (February 15, 1942), no access to allotment gardening (March 22, 1938). On the other hand, rigorous thought control: racial studies were to be taught in grade school (September 13, 1933), all Jewish men had to add the name Israel, all women Sara (August 17, 1938).

One by one the professions were closed to Jews: school teachers (date shockingly early: April 1, 1933, two months after the Nazis took power), judges (March 31, 1933), dentists (January 17, 1939), veterinarians (January 17, 1939), midwives (December 21, 1938), managers (November 12, 1938), authors (March 1935: but what does it mean to forbid writers from writing?). A whole set of exclusions is aimed precisely at the professions most closely linked with this community: publishers and booksellers (December 1938), doctors (July 25, 1938), art and antique dealers (1935), musicians (March 31, 1935), study at universities (April 15, 1937), retail stores (November 12, 1938). It's like a roster of what Berlin's Jews had contributed to the life of the metropolis.

However cunning and disturbing this display of texts, there is something far more *unheimlich* in the mix. Each of the eighty signs has two faces, the words on one side, and a picture on the other. How to describe these jaunty, engaging, brightly colored images that form the obverse of every horror message scattered through the neighborhood? They variously suggest diagrams, manifestoes, advertisements: call it diabolical Pop Art, eighty mini-Warhols for the streets of the city that brought us the Holocaust. The culinary representations, for instance, are all luscious to the eye: the crusty loaf of bread against a glowing teal background that illustrates the decree that Jews have only one hour a day in which to buy food; the palpably chewable bunch of radishes attached to the law against Jews doing allotment gardening; the exquisitely decorated layer cake, complete with pink doily, on the back of the ban on Jews buying sweets. It's like a sales pitch for a product you're forbidden to acquire. There are other sales pitches: a trio of dress shirts placed on an alluring diagonal (Jews may not own retail shops) or a string of pearls on a velour-colored background (Jews must hand over their jewelry). Quite often, it's the world as seen through the eyes of the very young: the chalk diagram of hopscotch on the back of the injunction against Jews and non-Jews playing together, or the child's drawing of a happy little house (with a high Bavarian-style gable) that illustrates the limitation on Jews inheriting property. On one occasion, however, there is complete blackness; the text on the reverse: "The emigration of Jews is forbidden. October 23, 1941."

Every one of these little signs tells a story—indeed, many stories, including those in the experience of twenty-first-century observers. One in particular I recall witnessing, though it was so silent that I'm not sure what story it told. As I was making my regular pathways through the Bayerisches Viertel one day, I stopped at some distance from one of the Stih-Schnock installations. Ahead of me on one side of the sign was a young mother staring at "Jews are no longer allowed to have household pets. February 15, 1942"; on the other side of the sign was her five- or six-year-old daughter looking up delightedly at the gorgeous rendering of a plump calico cat. They remained in this symmetrical posture for maybe ten seconds. Were there conversations between them afterwards? If so, the artists have done their job. I doubt that the millions spent on the Jewish Museum or the Holocaust Memorial—with all due respect—would have done it any better.

I suppose the reason that I find this Place of Remembrance, as it's called, the most evocative of all the remembrances is that one has to go looking for it, perhaps even get lost as one follows it through the neighborhood. Which makes it a kind of memorial version of Benjamin's losing himself in the city. With that in mind, a final story, closer to home than the encounter I witnessed between mother and daughter.

One summer afternoon in Berlin-Charlottenburg, after a lunch at our favorite Chinese restaurant, my spouse and I decided that we would attempt to retrace Walter Benjamin's erring steps away from home and toward the rendezvous with that unloved distant relative who was to accompany him to Rosh Hashanah services. This was no easy historical re-creation. The identity of the relative is lost to history, as is his domicile, if indeed that was place where they were to meet. On the other hand, we could be relatively certain about the starting point: from ages 12 to 19, Walter lived with his family at Carmerstraße 3, where a grand private home of early twentieth-century vintage still stands.

Which left the synagogue that stood at the end of the wayward journey that, as Benjamin tells it, gave birth to the idea of sexual satisfaction in the streets. The best help we could get from him is that it was "in all likelihood" a Reform Congregation, but that note of vagueness—no reason that he would be certain after all those years, especially since he never got there—kept multiple options open. We began our campaign carefully, calculating an upper limit of half an hour's walk. Marking that radius on the map, and focusing on the westerly direction, we came up with three possibilities. Admittedly, we were a bit cavalier about the dates when these houses of worship came into operation. Given the growth spurt of new synagogues in the very years of Benjamin's childhood, we couldn't be certain of nailing the matter down; on the other hand, we knew we were just playing a history game. So, selecting the closest of the possible end points for reenacting the momentous voyage, a Liberal synagogue in Pestalozzistraße, we renounced the aid of GPS (since the boy clearly had no map), and we started moving west. I should add that, given the frequency of our stays in Berlin and our fondness for that particular Chinese restaurant, we think we know the area pretty well.

Not so, it turned out. We enjoyed considerable advantages over young Walter—we had, for instance, some years previously actually been to the Pestalozzistraße synagogue, though it was for years under restoration—and we completed the first stages of our journey with great confidence. I won't say that we had fully mastered the cracking twigs and the mountain hollows of Knesebeckstraße—more like taken note of a Spanish wine shop and an Indian take-away—but we were feeling quite superior to the twelve-year-old whose footsteps we were attempting to follow. Then, just where we expected to debouch into Pestalozzistraße, there was no Pestalozzistraße. Instead, we found ourselves clueless at a seemingly normal 90° street corner where we had no idea whether to go left, right, or straight on through. Whereupon we abandoned the project of hunting for the other synagogues.

The reasons for our confusion—easily discerned once we resorted to the Blackberry—are not very remarkable: Carmerstraße appears to be on a rectangular grid but in fact it's one of the spokes of a fan, and Pestalozzistraße keeps itself separate from that particular geometry. But the experience of losing our way *was* remarkable. We had failed to reenact one particular urban walk, but we had caught a glimpse of that grander version of being lost on the streets of a city. Or, to put the matter of that unidentified synagogue another way, Walter never got there, we never got there, and we were probably looking in the wrong place anyway.

Absence probably tells the story best. It's this persistent thread of denial, of a Judaism that leaves a space within it, willingly or unwillingly, for not-Judaism, that makes Berlin my epicenter. Granted, there are Jews in Berlin. A tiny number never left, a small number chose to return, both of these being very aging populations. There is also immigration—we're told that Germany has the fastest-growing Jewish community in the world, though the discipline of statistics teaches us that if you start from near-zero, you're bound to have rapid growth—and, as any visitor is bound to notice, there is enough klezmer and Heine and (as we've seen) monumental remembrances to make forgetting very difficult. Still, I don't think anyone would seriously contest the proposition that the main thing about Jews in Berlin is that they aren't here. Of course, if you look at those familiar aerial photographs of the city from 1945, you might also say that the main thing about Berlin is that Berlin isn't here.

So whatever version of the city and whatever populations we're talking about, Berlin is bound to be a place of ruin, loss, absence, and the need for reconstruction, material or virtual, with the help of historical imaginations. Walter Benjamin, especially in writing about his early life, sets just the right example for us. Think of it as one of those formal analogies. Just as Benjamin is exiled from the city of his childhood without possibility of return, so we stand in relation to that remarkable flowering of European civilization that took place on this same land mass in the nineteenth and early twentieth centuries—for instance, the Enlightenment and early romanticism of Rahel Varnhagen and the civic and aesthetic generosities of James Simon, along with the traces of that culture to be glimpsed in Schönhauser Allee or the Bavarian Quarter. We are exiled from all this not just because the past is always past, though that's true as well, but because the physical Berlin of all that culture, along with many of its inhabitants, was largely obliterated. Still, we can do what Benjamin could not do, and what I urge you to do: we can actually walk the streets of this city—haunted, but also honored, by an indelible past.

Acknowledgments

This book would not have been written without the affectionate collaboration of a host of friends and colleagues who led me to visit, to understand, and to love the city. Stephen Greenblatt first brought me to Berlin with an invitation to lecture at the Wissenschaftskolleg; for that and many other acts of friendship over half a century, I am immensely grateful. A fellowship at the American Academy in Berlin in 2009–10 sealed the deal of my attachment to the city. That meant, above all, the incomparable executive director, Gary Smith, whose colleagueship and encouragement gave me some of my first opportunities to become a *Berliner* (or better, a *Wahlberliner*—a Berliner-by-choice). Much gratitude as well to some of my fellow Fellows at the Academy: David Abraham, Rick Atkinson, Nathan Englander, Janet Gezari, Joel Harrington, Susan Howe, Peter Maass, and Andrew Norman. A later stay in Berlin, during which I completed this book, brought me to the Institut für Kunst- und Bildgeschichte at the Humboldt University, where I had the privilege of working alongside Horst Bredekamp, whom I am honored to consider both colleague and friend. An equally stimulating educational institution was the dinner table of Renata Stih and Frieder Schnock, where pleasure, wisdom, and taste constituted the joyous curriculum. The year also produced and nourished some extraordinary friendships that deepened my sense of belonging in Berlin. A mere alphabetical listing hardly does them justice; with apologies, then: Patrick Baker, Daniela Comani, Katrin Grote-Baker, Klaus Hentges, Tarek Ibrahim, Marielouise Janssen-Jurreit, Daniel Kehlmann, Miriam Kellerhals, Anna Leube, Quincy Liu, Isabelle Lorenz, Uwe Luedemann, Jost Muxfeldt, Christoph Niemann, Georg Nolte, Anne Rubesame, Beate Söntgen, Tim Standaert, Olga Stein, Stefan Trinks, Stefan Vinzberg, Josef Vogl, Ittai

Weinryb, Lisa Zeitz, Claudia Ziegeler. Warm thanks as well to the very talented Andrew Miller, who—despite his self-definition as "a *goy* who has never been to Berlin"—drew the maps that adorn this volume.

Deepest gratitude of all to my favorite *Wahlberliner* and indispensable companion in all life's travels, Nick Barberio.

Suggestions for Further Reading

The bibliography of materials on Jews, Germans, and Berlin is nearly infinite; herewith is a brief selection of particularly informative works that can guide readers who wish to pursue these subjects further.

Histories

Elon, Amos. *The Pity of It All: A Portrait of the German-Jewish Epoch, 1743–1933.*

Gay, Peter. *Weimar Culture: The Outsider as Insider.*

———. *My German Question: Growing up in Nazi Berlin.*

Gay, Ruth. *The Jews of Germany: A Historical Portrait.*

Hertz, Deborah. *How Jews Became Germans: The History of Conversion and Assimilation in Berlin.*

———. *Jewish High Society in Old Regime Berlin.*

Mosse, W. E. *The German Jewish Economic Elite 1820–1935: A Socio-Cultural Profile.*

Nachama, Andreas, Julius Schoeps, and Hermann Simon. *Jews in Berlin.*

Stern, Fritz. *Dreams and Delusions: The Drama of German History.*

———. *Gold and Iron: Bismarck, Bleichröder, and the Building of the German Empire.*

Guides

Hörner, Unda. *Orte Jüdischen Lebens in Berlin: Literarische Spaziergänge durch Mitte.*

Nachama, Andreas, and Ulrich Eckhardt. *Jüdische Orte in Berlin.*

Rebiger, Bill. *Jewish Berlin: Culture, Religion, Daily Life Yesterday and Today.*

Roth, Andrew, and Michael Frajman. *The Goldapple Guide to Jewish Berlin.*

Places

Blankenburg, Gudrun. *Das Bayerische Viertel in Berlin Schöneberg: Leben in einem Geschichtsbuch.*
Etzold, Alfred. *Die jüdischen Friedhöfe in Berlin.*
Jewish Community of Berlin. *The Jewish Cemetery Schönhauser Allee, Berlin*
Jüdisches Adressbuch für Gross-Berlin Ausgabe 1931 (reprinted 1994).
Köhler, Rosemarie, and Ulrich Kratz-Whan. *Der Jüdische Friedhof Schönhauser Allee*
Orte des Erinnerns: Jüdisches Alltagsleben im Bayerischen Viertel.
Twardawa, Susanne. *Viktoria-Luise-Platz.*

People

RAHEL VARNHAGEN

Arendt, Hannah. *Rahel Varnhagen: The Life of a Jewess.*
Bilski, Emily, and Emily Braun. *Jewish Women and Their Salons: The Power of Conversation.*
Hahn, Barbara. *Rahel Levin Varnhagens Briefwechsel.*
Thomann Tewarson, Heidi. *Rahel Levin Varnhagen: The Life and Work of a German Jewish Intellectual.*
Varnhagen, Rahel. *Rahel: Ein Buch des Andenkens für Ihre Freunde.*
Wilhelmy-Dollinger, Petra. *Die Berliner Salons.*

JAMES SIMON

Donath, Adolf. "Der Berliner Kaufmann als Kunstfreund," in *Der Aufstieg Berlins zur Weltstadt*, edited by M. Osborn.
Girardet, Cella-Margaretha. *Jüdische Mäzene für die Preußischen Museen.*
Matthes, Olaf. *James Simon: Mäzen im Wilhelminischen Zeitalter.*

Mosse, W. E. "Wilhelm II and the Kaiserjuden: A Problematical Encounter," in J. Reinharz and W. Schatzberg, *The Jewish Response to German Culture.*

Schultz, Berndt. *James Simon: Philanthropist and Patron of the Arts.*

WALTER BENJAMIN

Benjamin, Walter. *Berlin Childhood around 1900.*

———. *The Arcades Project.*

———. "A Berlin Chronicle," in *Selected Writings,* vol. 2, part 2.

Eiland, Howard, and Michael W. Jennings. *Walter Benjamin: A Critical Life.*

Hessel, Franz. *Ein Flâneur in Berlin.*

Scholem, Gershom. *Walter Benjamin: The Story of a Friendship.*